THE MAN BOOK

THE MAN BOOK

OTTO DeFay

 ST. MARTIN'S GRIFFIN ✖ NEW YORK

THE MAN BOOK. Copyright © 2008 by Otto DeFay. All rights reserved. Printed in the United States of America. For information, address St. Martin's Press, 175 Fifth Avenue, New York, N.Y. 10010.

www.stmartins.com

Book design by Phil Mazzone

Illustrations by Wendy Letven

Library of Congress Cataloging-in-Publication Data

DeFay, Otto.
    The man book / Otto DeFay.—1st St. Martin's Griffin ed.
        p. cm.
    ISBN-13: 978-0-312-38312-1
    ISBN-10: 0-312-38312-6
    1. Men—Life skills guides.   2. Men—Psychology.   I. Title.
HQ1090.D25   2008
646.70081—dc22

                                                2008009149

10   9   8

Dedicated to my grandfather, Ron, who taught me about
everything in this book

CONTENTS

ACKNOWLEDGMENTS

THE MATERIAL IN THIS book is either my original writing or is made up of data compiled from numerous sources. Some of it came my way via e-mails, jokes I was told, or arguments I was in. A lot of it was developed while doing my job as a sports-data analyst. Overall, it was written down day-in and day-out whenever I came across something that every guy ought to know.

I can't take credit for all of the jokes in here—since some of them have been around forever—but if you happen to be the inventor of a particular joke in these pages, let me know and I'll be happy to buy you a round of beers.

Thanks to my agent, Ken, and Marc and Sarah over at St. Martin's. They made this book a reality. If not for them, you'd be reading blank pages.

A bunch of guys came up with ideas that I've included in this book, so they deserve mention here, as well as a shot of tequila when the royalty check comes in.

Randall Glenn, Ward Eddy, Thom Leelah, Patrick

Jameson, Jon Roberto, Joseph Micah, and past and present members of the X-Treme & X-Pensive Sports League: John Michaelson, the Two Professors, Brooksie, Pat Daniello, Tuckman, Rich Mitchell, Hose, Woj Mahal, Beery, and Pete Christopher.

Once you're done reading this book, the manliness continues over at www.ottodefay.com, where I'm running a blog related to everything from sports to sex. Feel free to add your comments about stuff you like or stuff that pisses you off. See you there.

And finally, thanks for reading this book.

—ODF

THE MAN BOOK

INTRODUCTION

YOU ARE A MAN. This is your book.

This is a book for males. More specifically, men. There are hundreds, if not thousands, of books for women and for girls. They address the needs of a woman's body, of a woman's emotional self, of a woman's relationship with her mother, of a woman's desire to go shopping. Chances are, one or more of these has already found its way into your home.

However, there has not been a single book—not one—about men and men's bodies, men's emotions, and all the things that go into becoming a man.

First of all, the idea sounds silly. Or perhaps even downright stupid. Men don't want to hear about such things. Men grow up, and they deal with it. That is the essence of being a man.

Unfortunately, growing up is never as easy as it's supposed to be. Men do have problems with their bodies. Men do have emotions. And, much as they don't want to admit, men have needs. Those needs extend beyond sports, sex, and alcohol. Not far, but they do extend.

We're not here to get all touchy-feely. Quite the contrary, we're here to provide information, some of it amusing, some of it scientific, some of it useful, some of it trivial. All of it is designed to be read while waiting for your significant other in the dress department of the local department store. Or perhaps while you're spending quality time in the bathroom after a night of eating jalapeño bratwursts and chili dogs.

Women's books have names like *Our Bodies, Ourselves, Growing a Girl, Reviving Ophelia,* and Martha Stewart's *Entertaining.* Men don't have books—they have magazines. Most of these magazines you can't read in public after the age of thirty. Certainly, they're not the kind of magazines that your significant other is going to appreciate you leaving on the coffee table just as she is getting ready to have a baby shower for her best friend.

So it's time for a book. This book.

This book is for men. Certainly, adolescent males will find much of interest—and much to laugh about—in these pages. Finding humor in just about everything is part of becoming a man. But our target male is not just the man who is in the mood to laugh, but someone who might be on his way to getting married, is already married, or equally important, has just scheduled his first prostate exam.

No one ever tells a growing man his nipples will hurt if he bumps them during gym in high school, that his pubic hairs will turn gray one at a time, or that someday sleep will be more desirable than sex.

No one ever tells you. So we're going to.

And we're not going to stop there. For instance, no one ever quite knows how big a soccer field should be. We do.

No one gives you that perfect joke to tell the boss when he's treating you like his best friend. We do.

No one tells you how big your girlfriend's tits really are. We do.

No one quite remembers who won the NASCAR championship ten years ago, or what the exact difference is between a single malt and blended whiskey, or how to make a martini, or what a petabyte is, or Iron Man's secret identity, or the difference between hail and sleet, or what to buy for a twentieth anniversary, or the best things to say during a prostate exam.

We do.

Be a man. Read on.

A THOUSAND NAMES FOR YOUR PENIS (NOT COUNTING PENIS)

A

ace in the hole • acorn Andy • Adam halfpint • Admiral Winky • AIDS grenade • the Alabama blacksnake • albino cave dweller • all-day sucker • anaconda • anal impaler • anal intruder • anal spear • ankle spanker • apple-headed monster • ass blaster • ass pirate • ass wedge • auger-headed gut wrench

B

baby maker • baby's arm holding an apple • baby's arm in a boxing glove • bacon bazooka • bacon rod • bad boy • bagpipe • Bald Avenger • the bald-headed beauty • bald-headed giggle stick • bald-headed hermit • bald-headed Jesus • bald-headed yogurt slinger • bald-headed spunk-juice dispenser • ball buddy • baloney pony • banana • battering ram • bayonet • Bavarian beefstick • beanstalk • beard splitter • beastus maximus • beaver buster • Beaver Cleaver • bed flute • bed snake • beef baton • beef bayonet • beef bugle • beef bus • beef missile • beef soldier • beef stick • Beefy McManstick • bell rope • belly stick • best leg of three • (big) beanpole • big Jake the one-eyed snake • big Jim and the twins • big Johnson • Big Lebowski • big number one • Big Red • big rod • big uncle • biggus dickus • Bilbo Baggins • bishop • the bishop with his nice red hat • bitch blaster • bitch stick • bits and pieces • blind butler • blind snake • blood blunt • blood slug • blood sword • Blow Pop • blowtorch • blue steel • blue-veined jackhammer • blue-veined junket pumper • blue-veined piccolo • blue-veined custard chucker • blue-veiner • blunt • Bob • Bob Johnson • bobo • bone • bone phone • bone a phone • bone roller-coaster • boneless beef • boneless fish • boner • bone-her • bop gun • bottle rocket • bowlegged swamp donkey • box buster • boy brush • bradford and the pair • bratwurst • breakfast burrito • breakfast wood • broom • Brutus • bubba • bulbous big-knob • bumtickler • bush beater • bush rusher • bushwhacker • Buster Hymen • Buster McThunderstick • butt blaster • butt pirate • butter churn • butter knife

C

candy cane • caped crusader • Captain Bilbo • Captain Crook • Captain Hook • Captain Howdy • Captain Kirk • Captain Winky • carnal stump • cattle prod • cave hunter • cax • cervix crusader • cervix pounder • chancellor • the chap • Charlie Russell the one-eyed muscle • cheese staff • cherry picker • cherry-poppin' daddy • cherry splitter • Chi Zi Wang • chick sticker • chicksicle • chief of staff • chimbo • chimney cleaner • choo-choo • choad (chode) • chorizo • chowder dumper • chubby • chubby conquistador • chum •

chunk o' love • chunder thunder • cigar • circus boy •
clam digger • clam hammer • clam sticker • clit tickler •
clown • the cob • cock • cock goblin • cocktus • cockus
erectus • codger • colon cowboy • colon crusader •
colossus • command module • coral branch • corned
beef lighthouse • corn dog • cornholer • cornstalk •
cornstalk cowboy • crack hunter • crack smacker •
cramstick • crank • crank shaft • cream-filled meat
stick • cream bandit • cream cannon • creamsicle •
creamstick • cream spritzer • crimson chitterling • crimson Darth Vader • crippler • crotch cobra • crotch cowboy • crotch rocket • crotch vomiter • crushin' Russian •
the cum pump • cummingtonite • cunny-catcher • cunt
caper • the cunt companion • cunt pumper • cunt rifle •
cunt scrubber • Cupid's arrow • Curious George • custard cannon • custard pump • cyclops

D

daddy long-stroke • danglin' fury • danglin' wang •
dangling participle • dart of love • Darth Vader • Davy
Crockett • deep-veined purple-helmeted spartan of love •
demeanor • the diamond cutter • dick • Dick and his two
swingers • Dick and the twins • dickimus maximus • dick-
ory dock • dickory-smoked coal sausage • digit • diller •
dilly-ho-ho • ding-a-ling • ding-dong • dingle • dingle
dangle • dingledong • dinglehopper • dingus • dingy •
dinky • dipstick • Dirk Diggler • divining rod • dobber •
docking tube • dolphin • dong • dong-bong • dong-stick •
dongle • donker • Donkey Kong • doodad • doo-dah • doodle • doodle dandy • dooker • doohickey • doppelganger •
dork • doughnut holder • dribbling dart of love • dribbling

dragon • Dr. Cyclops • Dr. Feelgood • Dr. Wang • Duke •
dumb stick • dungula bone

E

early riser • earthworm Jim • easy rider • egg roll • eight
inches of throbbing pink Jesus • equipment • El Capitan •
El Presidente • elastic plastic • elephant trunk • Elmer
the glue shooter • Elvis • engine cranker • everlasting
gob-dropper • every-other-time • excreting eel • executive staff member

F

family jewels • fandangle • Fat Albert • fat finger • fat
Johnson • fetus feeler • fiddle bow • fiddle stick • fire-
breathing dragon • fire hose • fire rod • fireman Ed • firm
worm • Fishhook • fishing rod • fishing tackle • flapdoo-
dle • fleshbone • flesh bat • flesh enema • flesh flute • flesh
hoagie • flesh injection • flesh maggot • flesh pistol • flesh
rocket • flesh tornado • flesh trumpet • flesh twinkie •
fleshy Winnebago • flip-flap • fluid spitter • foaming beef
probe • foo-foo • foofer (foof) • fool sticker • footlong •
fondo worm • frank 'n' beans • frankfurter • Freddy fire-
hose • Freddy fish monger • Free Willy • frigamajig •
frightful hog • fuck flute • fuck puppet • fuckpole • fuck-
stick • fudgepacker • full meal • fun gun • fun truncheon •
fury • fuzzbuster

G

gadget • gag mallet • gap stopper • gash mallet • gearshift •
general • German soldier • gherkin • giant-sized man-
thing • giggle stick • gimmer stick • Girthy McGirth •

girthy sausage • giving tree • gleaming love sword • glo worm • gluestick • Godzilla • goo pipe • goose's neck • governor • Grabthar's hammer • Grandpa's knee • granite edifice • gravy maker • great pyramid • grinding tool • guided muscle • gummi worm • gushin' Prussian • gut buster • gut stick • gut tapper • gut wrench guy

H

hairy pencil • hair splitter • Hairy Houdini • Hairy Scary and the two bald men • ham roll • hammer of Thor • Hampton • handfucker • handgun • handwarmer • Handy Andy • hang-lo • hanging chad • hanging hag • hanging Johnny • happy worm • hard-on • hardware • Harry • Harry & the Hendersons • Harry hot dog • he-ham • he-man sword • he who must be obeyed • heat-seeking moisture missile • helmet man • Herbie • Herculean lizard • Herman the one-eyed German • Herman von Longschlongstein • hidden treasure • high pressure vein cane • his eminence • his majesty • his rig • hog • hog leg • hole cork • holy poker • holy water sprinkler • home wrecker • honeypot cleaver • honey stick • Honk the magic goose • hoo hoo • hooded warrior • hooty hoo • horse-necked clam • hose • hot beef injection • hot dog • hot popsicle • hot tamale • Hugo • humdiddler • Hung Wei Lo • hunka-hunka burnin' love • hymen hammer

I

ice cream machine • impregnator • incredible bulk • inflatable iron • injection erection • instant sex drive lever • Inter Cuntinental Ballistic Missile • intrusion protrusion • invincible man • iron horse • iron rod • Italian stallion • itty bitty meat • Ivan the Terrible • ivory shaft

J

Jack in the box • jackhammer • Jake the one-eyed snake • javelin • jellyfish • jerkin' gherkin • jibberstick • jigger • jiggling bone • Jim and the twins • Jiminy Cricket • Jimmy • Jimmy Wriggler • jing jang • jingle bone • jizz syringe • jizz whiz • jockey stick • Johnson • John Thomas • John Thursday • Johnny Come Early • joint • JoJo the circus clown • jolly green giant • jolly jellybean • joyprong • joystick • Julio • junior • junk

K

Kaptain Kielbasa • Ken Cracker • Kentucky horn • Kentucky telescope • Kibbles 'n Bits • kickstand • kidney cracker • kidney scraper • kielbasa • king • King Dingaling • King Dong • the kipper ripper • knee knocker • knowledge stick • knob • Kojak • Komodo dragon • Kong • kosher pickle

L

lady dagger • lance of love • lap rope • leaky faucet • leather lollipop • Lewinski lunch • lickin' stick • licorice stick • life preserver • lil' buddy • lil' Mister • Lincoln log • little admiral • the little bastard • little Billy • little bishop in a turtleneck • little brother • little colonel • little Dickie • little Dutch boy • little Elvis • little friend • little gator • little guy • little Jesus • little Juan • little man • little shepherd boy • little slugger • little Willy • live sausage • lizard • lobster • lollipop • Long Dong Silver • long John • long Tom • Longrod Von Hugenstein • Lord James D'Armais • Lord Plumber • Louisville plugger • Louisville slugger • love gun • love leg • love log • love lollipop • love meat • love muscle • love-n-ator • the love pole • love pump • love sausage • love stick • love sub • love sword • love thruster • love train • love trunchcon • love wand • love weasel • love whistle • love torpedo • lucky Chucky • lunch • lunchmeat truncheon • lung disturber • lung puncturer • (luscious) lollipop

M

magenta mushroom • magic Johnson • magic member • magic wand • main vein • Major Manchowder • Major Woody • man-dingler • man-milk dispenser • man-child • mangina • mangroin • manimal • man axe • man cannon • man hammer • man loaf • man log • man meat • man muscle • man pipe • man plow • man pole • man root • man's best friend • marriage tackle • marrowbone • master blaster • Master John Goodfellow • master of ceremonies • Master Wang • mayonnaise cannon • mayonnaise pistol • maypole • meat • meat 'n' potatoes • meat 'n' (two) veggies • meat balloon • meat bat • meat cigar • meat flute • meat hammer • meat missile • meat musket • meat pipe • meat pole • meat popsicle • meat puppet • meat skewer • meat speculum • meat stick • meat straw • meat thermometer • meat train • meat whistle • meat wrench • meaty cudgel • meaty internal spine support • meaty tongue depressor • melon baster • member • menstrual miner • Midas • middle leg • midnight wangler • mighty anaconda • mighty Dolan • mighty Joe Young • mighty monkey • mighty Thor • the milkman • Mini-Me • mister • mister happy • Moby Dick • mojo • molten mushroom • monkeymaker • monkey • monkey tamer • monster • Monty's python • morning muscle • Moses • Mr. Bendy • Mr. Big • Mr. Bigglesworth • Mr. Bo • Mr. Boing Boing • Mr. Bojangles • Mr. Clean • Mr. Eel-y • Mr. Friendly • Mr. Giggles • Mr. Happy • Mr. Jiggle Daddy • Mr. Johnson and the juice crew • Mr. Magoo • Mr. Merrymaker • Mr. Microphone • Mr. Mojo Risin' • Mr. Mouth Missle • Mr. Mushroom Head • Mr. Pee-pee • Mr. Peepers • Mr. Potato Head • Mr. President • Mr. Rogers • Mr. Salami • Mr. Sniffles • Mr. Toad's wild ride • Mr. Wiggles • Mr. Wigglestick • Mr. Wiggly • Mr. Willy • Mr. Winky • Mr. Wobbly • muff marauder • muffin butterer • mule • murky lurker • muscle of love • mushroom on a stick • mushroom-tipped love dart • mustn'-touchit • mutton dagger • mutton javelin • mutton pole • muzzled bulldog

N

nail • Navajo hogan • the Nebuchadnezzar • needle • nightcrawler • nightstick • nimrod • nine-inch knocker • nuke

O

old one-eye • old blind Bob • old chap • old drizzly • Old Faithful • old fella • old man • old slimy • Oliver Twist •

one-eyed bathtub eel • one-eyed blue-vein • one-eyed Charlie and the stink twins • one-eyed cornhusker • one-eyed cow killer • one-eyed custard chucker • one-eyed Fred • one-eyed giant • one-eyed gopher • one-eyed hip snake • one-eyed horny newt • one-eyed Jack • one-eyed milkman • one-eyed moisture missle • one-eyed monster • one-eyed nightcrawler • one-eyed snake • one-eyed superhero • one-eyed throbbing python of love • one-eyed trouser mouse • one-eyed trouser psychic • one-eyed trouser snake • one-eyed trouser trout • one-eyed Willy • one-eyed wonder weasel • one-eyed wonder worm • one-eyed wrinkle-necked trouser trout • one-eyed yogurt thrower • one-holed bologna phone • one-holed friction whistle • one hundred percent all-beef thermometer • one-string bass • Optimus Prime • organ • other head • Otis Deepthroatis • our one-eyed brother • ovarian pool stick • oyster probe

P

package • pajama python • Palm Pilot • Panda Express • pants snake • papa's poker • passion pistol • passion pump • peacemaker • peanut • pearl diver • pearl pole • Pebbles and Bam Bam • pecker • Pedro • pee-pee • Pee-Wee • peener • peenie • pelvic punisher • pelvis thumb • pencil • pendulum • peni • penial • Pennis the Menace • Pepe • Peppito • Percy • perpendicular pickle • the Pete(r) • Peter the Great • petit Jesu • phallus • piccolo • pickle • pied piper • piece • piece of pork • pig in a blanket • pigskin bus • pigsticker • pikestaff • pile driver • pillipacker • pimp cane • pimpin' stick • pink cigar •

Pink Floyd • pink oboe • pink-seeking missile • pink torpedo • pinkle • pipe cleaner • piss pump • piss handle •
piss whistle • pisser • piston rod • placenta poker • pleasure missile • pleasure pickle • pleasure piston • plonker
• pocket pool stick • pocket rocket • Polish kielbasa •
polished pine • plum-tree shaker • pocket otter • pocket
perch • pocket rocket • Poka-her-hontas • pogo stick •
pointer • pole • polvo • polyphemus • pompadoodle •
poon farmer • poon prod • poon wrecker • poontanger •
poozle weasel (woozle) • Pope John Pole III • Popeye •
porcelain plumber • porridge gun • pork knife • pork
sword • pork truncheon • porkeroon • porksicle • porn
prong • porridge pump • power rod • power prawn •
premeditator • presidential podium • prick • prickolo •
pride and joy • primus pilus • Prince Charming • Prince
Everhard of the Netherlands • private parts • probe •
prong • protein spicket • protein torpedo • pube kabob •
pubic bong • pud • Puff the Magic Dragon • pulsating
python of love • pulsating woodwind • pump-action
yogurt rifle • pump handle • pumping pole of penile
power • pup tent • puppet Jack • purple avenger •
purple bulb • purple-headed bed snake • purple-headed
belly ripper • purple-headed cum shooter • purple-
headed custard chucker • purple-headed love truncheon •
purple-headed meat scepter • purple-headed pirate •
purple-headed punisher • purple-headed warrior •
purple-headed womb broom • purple-headed womb ferret • purple-headed yogurt slinger • purple-helmeted
soldier of love • purple-helmeted Nazi of love • purple-
helmeted warrior • purple muffin • purple mushroom •
purple pile driver • purple pork chop • purple pulsating

pillar of power • pussy duster • pussy piston • pussy plumber • pussy plunger • pussy poker • pussy pounder • pussy stretcher • pud • putz

Q

quarter master • quarter pounder with cheese • quick-shot Sam • quim-tickler • quivering member

R

rainbow roll • Ralph the fur-faced chicken • ramburglar • ramrod • ranger • real deal • Reaming Tower of Penis • red ender • red-helmeted love warrior • red-hot poker • red rocket • rhubarb • Richard and the twins • Richard Cranium • Richard Head • Rick Hard • ring stinger • rising cedar • rocket to Uranus • rod • rod hard ride • rod of lordly might • Rodney Stickshift • Rodzilla • rogering ramjet • rolling pin • Roman soldier • root • root of all evil • Roto-Rooter • round steak • ruby-headed love dart • ruddy sausage • rump wrangler • Rumpleforeskin • Russell the love muscle • Russell the one-eyed (wonder) muscle

S

salami • salami grande • salty dog • sausage roll • scabby mayonnaise revolver • scepter • schlong • Schlongmaster 2000 • schnickel • schnitzel • schvance/schvantz • schvontz/schwantz • Schwartz • Scooby snack • schlort • schmeckle • schmuck • seed shooter • Señor Happy • Sergeant Stiffy • serpentine • sex pistol • shaft • shaft of Cupid • sheep shank • sheep shifter • shift stick • shit hook • shit stick • short arm • shrimp boat • silk shocker • silly Willy's stick of mayhem • single-bore mayonnaise pistol • Sir Martin Wagstaff • Sir Spanks-a-Lot • six shooter • skin boat • skin bus • skin diver • skin flute • skivvies lizard • skippy • Sleeping Beauty • Slick Dilly • Slim Jim • slim reaper • the slippery love dolphin • slit-eyed demon • slong • sludge pump • slut stick • snappy beef stick • snot sausage • soldier • solicitor general • soul pole • soup can • sour cream rifle • snake • snapper slapper • snoz wanger • spackle hammer • spam dagger • spam javelin • spanky • spelunker • spelunking sausage • sperm burper • sperm spitter • spermin' Herman • sper-minator • spigot • spike bit • spitting python • spitting snake • split-ass mechanic • split-headed bishop • splooge moose • spongey-headed warrior • spoo shooter • sprout • spunk spitter • spunk stick • spunk trunk • spunker • Spurt Reynolds • squinty blowpop • squirmin' Herman the one-eyed German • staff • staff of life • stain maker • stallion • standing Hampton • Stanley • Stanley the power tool • stick o' salami • stick • stick shift • sticky shooter • stiff one-eye • stiff sausage • stiffy • stink ham-mer • stomach wrench • strawberry snake • stretchy and the twins • strumpet thumper • stubby • sugar stick • super schlong of love • suspect • sweet meat • swelling mushroom • swingin' death • swingin' Dick Nixon • swingin' sirloin • swizzle stick • swollen blood bomber

T

taco warmer • tally whacker • tank slapper • tapioca sprinkler • tassle • teeter • Tennessee throat warmer •

tent peg • tent pole • Texas trout banger • thadge naviga-
tor • thingamabob • thing(y) • third arm of justice •
third leg • Thomas • Thor's hammer • three-inch
punisher • the Three's Company • thrill drill • throat
choker • throbbing blood sword • throbbing horse cock •
throbbing purple pneumatic drill of love • throbbing
purple spear of destiny • throbbing python of love •
thumper • thunder stick • tickle tail • tickle Toby • tid-
dlywinker • tingler • Tinky Winky • tiny Elvis • Tiny Tim •
titmouse • Tobias the cheeky monkey • Tom Jones • Tom
Slick • Tonka • tonsil tickler • tool • tool of the patri-
archy • torch of Cupid • totem pole • tower of power •
tree of life • trembling torpedo • trombone • trouble-
maker • trouser flute • trouser hog • trouser Mauser •
trouser mouse • trouser snake • trouser tortoise • trouser
trombone • trouser trout • trout baster • tuba • tube
steak • tummy banana • tummy buster • tuna baster •
tuna fisher • the tunnel tickler • turgid member • turkey
neck • turtle • twat expander • twat torquer • twat
torpedo • twat washer • tweeder • twelve-inch train of
pain • twenty-first digit • twig • twig 'n' berries • twig 'n'
giggle berries • twinkie • twizzler of love • the two-legged
sword • two pebbles and a twig • two pounds of swinging
meat

U

ugly brother • ugly stick • Uncle Chunk • Uncle Dick •
Uncle Reamus • Uncle Richard • Uncle Spunk • Uncle
Throbby • Uncle Wiggly • unemployed • unit • upright
citizen • upright organ • upright uncle • uterus
unicorn

V

vagina miner • vaginal dilator • vaginal explorer • Vaseline machine gun • vein-laden meat pipe • vein-laden meat stick • veinous maximus • veiny bangstick • verga • vertical dangler • verve pipe • Viagra baby • vicious dink • virile member • Vlad the Impaler • vomit rod • vomiting dummy

W

wacker • Waldo • Wally • Wally the one-eyed wonder wiener • wand of light • wang • wanker • wanker spanker • war hammer • the waterspout • wazoo • wedding finger • wedding tackle • wedding wrecker • wedge bone • Ween • weenie • wee-wee • Wee Willy Winky • wee wonder stick • wenis • whamadoodle • whammy bar • whisker slitter • whistle • whistle stick • who-who • whopper • whore monger • whore pipe • whore thermometer • wicked scepter • widget • wiener • wife and kids • wife's best friend • wife's worst enemy • wigga wagga • wiggedy wang • wiggity wang • wiggle stick • wiggling worm • wilbert • Wilbur • Willard • Willy • Willy the one-eyed wonder worm • Willy Wonka • wing-wang • winkster • winky • Winky the milk-spitting tunnel ferret • wizard's staff • wobbly warhead • womb broom • womb hammer • womb raider • womb scud • womb warrior • wonder down under • wonder weiner • wonder wick • wong • wonga • wood • woodle • woody • wookie • worm in a roll-neck pullover • Wormy McJuicemaker • wriggling pole • wrinklebeast

X

Xcaliber • XTC Stick

Y

yam • yang • yard o' beef • ying yang • yogurt shooter • yogurt slinger • Yul Brynner • yum-yum • yummy hummer

Z

zamboner • Zamboni baloney • zapper wrench • zipper ripper • zipper trout • zipper wookie

• •

BREAST SIZES

Breast sizes are calculated by a combination of bra size and cup size. Here's the process:

1. **Bra size,** which is also called band size, is measured around the chest directly under the breasts with a cloth measuring tape. Add five inches to that measurement. If the bra size works out to an ODD number go up one inch to the next EVEN number. This dimension is the bra/band size and should equal the circumference around the chest, directly above the breasts/under the arms. Let's say the initial measurement is 32. Add five, you get 37. But bra

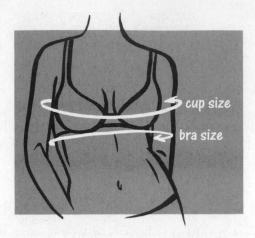

sizes are even numbers so round it up to 38. Therefore, the bra size is 38 inches.

2. **Cup Size** Next, measure around the chest at the
   fullest part of the breast. Let's say it's 42 inches.
   Now, subtract the bra size (38 inches, above) from
   this number. That gives you four inches difference.
   Four inches in cup size (according to chart, below)
   equals a D. Therefore, your lady is a 38D. By any
   measure, that's quite respectable. You should be
   proud.

DIFFERENCE	CUP SIZE		DIFFERENCE	CUP SIZE
Half inch	AA		Four inches	D
One inch	A		Five inches	DD or E
Two inches	B		Six inches	F
Three inches	C		Seven inches	G

Step-by-step example for those of you who didn't get it the first time:

STEP 1:   Underbust measurement is 37 inches. Add 5 inches. Bra size is 42.

STEP 2:   Full bust measurement is 45 inches.

STEP 3:   45–42 = 3-inch difference. Cup size is C.

RESULT: Your woman has 42C tits.

••••••••••••••••••••••••••••••

SCOTCH, WHISKEY, BOURBON & RYE

First off, Americans and the Irish spell whiskey with an "e," while the Scottish leave the "e" out. Scotch whisky, as you might guess, is whisky distilled in Scotland from barley malt. Irish whiskey is distilled in Ireland. Bourbon is whiskey that is distilled in the United States, and must be made from a mash that is not less than 51 percent corn grain. Rye is whiskey produced in the United States and Canada, and must be made from a mash that is not less than 51 percent rye grain. Most Canadian whiskeys are rye whiskeys.

Cognac is not related to whiskey—it's made from grapes.

SINGLE MALT VS. BLENDED SCOTCH WHISKY

A single malt Scotch whisky is the product of one specific distillery and has not been mixed with whisky from any other distilleries. There is also no other grain in the whisky; just a single barley malt. Most of the malt whisky distilleries are located in one of four regions in Scotland: Speyside, Highland, Lowland, and Cambeltown. Each of these regions has its own particular distinctive style of malt whisky.

A blended Scotch whisky may contain a combination of malt and grain whisky from over forty or fifty different malt and grain distilleries. The normal ratio of malt to grain is 40 percent malt to 60 percent grain. The percentage of malt used will determine the quality and smoothness of taste and character. Each whisky used in the blending process will normally have been matured for about five years, although there are a number of older blended scotch whiskies.

FOOTBALL FIELD POSITIONS

OFFENSE

Offensive players are linemen (seven players on the offensive line) or backs (four players in the backfield).

TYPICAL OFFENSIVE FORMATION:

(Linemen) split end / tackle / guard / center / guard / tackle / tight end quarterback

(Backs) halfback / fullback / halfback

DEFENSE

There are three elements of football defense: 1) the defensive line, 2) the linebackers, 3) the defensive backfield (also called the secondary).

Defensive alignments are categorized with two numbers. The first number is the number of players on the line; the second number is the number of linebackers. For example, teams may play a 5-3 defense (5 defensive linemen, 3 linebackers) or a 4-4 defense (4 defensive linemen, 4 linebackers).

TYPICAL 5-3 DEFENSIVE ALIGNMENT:

(Defensive linemen) end / tackle / nose guard / tackle / end

(Linebackers) outside linebacker / middle linebacker / outside linebacker

(Defensive backfield) cornerback / safety / cornerback

THE SUPER BOWL

XLII	2/3/2008	N.Y. Giants, 17	New England, 14
XLI	2/4/2007	Indianapolis, 29	Chicago, 17
XL	2/5/2006	Pittsburgh, 21	Seattle, 10
XXXIX	2/6/2005	New England, 24	Philadelphia, 21
XXXVIII	2/1/2004	New England, 32	Carolina, 29
XXXVII	1/26/2003	Tampa Bay, 48	Oakland, 21
XXXVI	2/3/2002	New England, 20	St. Louis, 17
XXXV	1/28/2001	Baltimore, 34	N.Y. Giants, 7
XXXIV	1/30/2000	St. Louis, 23	Tennessee, 16
XXXIII	1/31/1999	Denver, 34	Atlanta, 19
XXXII	1/25/1998	Denver, 31	Green Bay, 24
XXXI	1/26/1997	Green Bay, 35	New England, 21
XXX	1/28/1996	Dallas, 27	Pittsburgh, 17
XXIX	1/29/1995	San Francisco, 49	San Diego, 26
XXVIII	1/30/1994	Dallas, 30	Buffalo, 13
XXVII	1/31/1993	Dallas, 52	Buffalo, 17
XXVI	1/26/1992	Washington, 37	Buffalo, 24
XXV	1/27/1991	N.Y. Giants, 20	Buffalo, 19
XXIV	1/28/1990	San Francisco, 55	Denver, 10
XXIII	1/22/1989	San Francisco, 20	Cincinnati, 16
XXII	1/31/1988	Washington, 42	Denver, 10

XXI	1/25/1987	N.Y. Giants, 39	Denver, 20
XX	1/26/1986	Chicago, 46	New England, 10
XIX	1/20/1985	San Francisco, 38	Miami, 16
XVIII	1/22/1984	L.A. Raiders, 38	Washington, 9
XVII	1/30/1983	Washington, 27	Miami, 17
XVI	1/24/1982	San Francisco, 26	Cincinnati, 21
XV	1/25/1981	Oakland, 27	Philadelphia, 10
XIV	1/20/1980	Pittsburgh, 31	L.A. Rams, 19
XIII	1/21/1979	Pittsburgh, 35	Dallas, 31
XII	1/15/1978	Dallas, 27	Denver, 10
XI	1/9/1979	Oakland, 32	Minnesota, 14
X	1/18/1976	Pittsburgh, 21	Dallas, 17
IX	1/12/1975	Pittsburgh, 16	Minnesota, 6
VIII	1/13/1974	Miami, 24	Minnesota, 7
VII	1/14/1973	Miami, 14	Washington, 7
VI	1/16/1972	Dallas, 24	Miami, 3
V	1/17/1971	Baltimore, 16	Dallas, 13
IV	1/11/1970	Kansas City, 23	Minnesota, 7
III	1/12/1969	N.Y. Jets, 16	Baltimore, 7
II	1/14/1968	Green Bay, 33	Oakland, 14
I	1/15/1967	Green Bay, 35	Kansas City, 10

SUPER BOWL MVPS

1967 Super Bowl I: QB Bart Starr, Green Bay

1968 Super Bowl II: QB Bart Starr, Green Bay

1969 Super Bowl III: QB Joe Namath, N.Y. Jets

1970 Super Bowl IV: QB Len Dawson, Kansas City

1971 Super Bowl V: LB Chuck Howley, Dallas

1972 Super Bowl VI: QB Roger Staubach, Dallas

1973 Super Bowl VII: S Jake Scott, Miami

1974 Super Bowl VIII: RB Larry Csonka, Miami

1975 Super Bowl IX: RB Franco Harris, Pittsburgh

1976 Super Bowl X: WR Lynn Swann, Pittsburgh

1977 Super Bowl XI: WR Fred Biletnikoff, Oakland

1978 Super Bowl XII: DT Randy White and DE Harvey
   Martin, Dallas

1979 Super Bowl XIII: QB Terry Bradshaw, Pittsburgh

1980 Super Bowl XIV: QB Terry Bradshaw, Pittsburgh

1981 Super Bowl XV: QB Jim Plunkett, Oakland

1982 Super Bowl XVI: QB Joe Montana, San Francisco

1983 Super Bowl XVII: RB John Riggins, Washington

1984 Super Bowl XVIII: RB Marcus Allen, L.A. Raiders

1985 Super Bowl XIX: QB Joe Montana, San Francisco

1986 Super Bowl XX: DE Richard Dent, Chicago

1987 Super Bowl XXI: QB Phil Simms, NY Giants

1988 Super Bowl XXII: QB Doug Williams, Washington

1989 Super Bowl XXIII: WR Jerry Rice, San Francisco

1990 Super Bowl XXIV: QB Joe Montana, San Francisco

1991 Super Bowl XXV: RB Ottis Anderson, NY Giants

1992 Super Bowl XXVI: QB Mark Rypien, Washington

1993 Super Bowl XXVII: QB Troy Aikman, Dallas

1994 Super Bowl XXVIII: RB Emmitt Smith, Dallas

1995 Super Bowl XXIX: QB Steve Young, San Francisco
1996 Super Bowl XXX: CB Larry Brown, Dallas
1997 Super Bowl XXXI: KR Desmond Howard, Green Bay
1998 Super Bowl XXXII: RB Terrell Davis, Denver
1999 Super Bowl XXXIII: QB John Elway, Denver
2000 Super Bowl XXXIV: QB Kurt Warner, St. Louis
2001 Super Bowl XXXV: LB Ray Lewis, Baltimore
2002 Super Bowl XXXVI: QB Tom Brady, New England
2003 Super Bowl XXXVII: Dexter Jackson, Tampa Bay
2004 Super Bowl XXXVIII: QB, Tom Brady, New England
2005 Super Bowl XXXIX: WR, Deion Branch, New England
2006 Super Bowl XL: WR, Hines Ward, Pittsburgh
2007 Super Bowl XLI: QB, Peyton Manning, Indianapolis
2008 Super Bowl XLII: QB, Eli Manning, N.Y. Giants

The Most Valuable Player Award has been known as the Pete Rozelle Trophy since Super Bowl XXV.

• •

MOST IMPORTANT GUITARISTS

Duane Allman (Southern rock)
Chet Atkins (country)
Eric Clapton (blues rock)
Jeff Beck (rock, jazz, fusion)
Al Di Meola (jazz fusion)

Jimi Hendrix (rock)
Robert Johnson (blues)
Wes Montgomery (jazz)
Carlos Montoya (flamenco)
Jimmy Page (rock)
Jerry Reed (country)
Django Reinhart (jazz)
Andrés Segovia (classical)
Eddie Van Halen (rock)
Muddy Waters (blues)

• •

SPORTS FIELD AND COURT MEASUREMENTS

BASEBALL

Home plate to pitcher's rubber: 60'6"
    Home plate to second base: 127'3 3/8"
    Distance between bases: 90'

BASKETBALL

Court: 94' × 50'
    Free throw: 15' from face of backboard

FOOTBALL

Playing field: 100 yards × 53¾ yards
    End zone: 10 yards long, each

TENNIS

Court: 78'×27'
   Service line: 21' from net
   Net height: 3' in the center, 3'6" at posts

HANDBALL

Court: 34'×20'
   Service line: 16'

VOLLEYBALL

Court: 60'×30'
   Top of net from ground: 7'11⅝"

. . . .

POKER

Ranking of poker hands from best to worst.

ROYAL FLUSH

Ace, king, queen, jack, and 10—all of the same suit

STRAIGHT FLUSH

Five cards in numerical order, all of the same suit

FOUR OF A KIND

Four cards of the same face value, plus one other random card

FULL HOUSE

One pair and three of a kind, such as two 5s and three kings

FLUSH

Any five cards of the same suit

STRAIGHT

Five cards in numerical order, regardless of suit

THREE OF A KIND

Any three cards of the same face value, and two random cards

TWO PAIR

Two sets of pairs, and one other random card

ONE PAIR

Any two cards of the same face value, and three random cards

Note: Games played with wild cards can achieve five of a kind, which trumps all of the above.

THE BASICS OF WINE

Most wine, like just about every other alcohol, is an acquired taste. Here are some basics when you find yourself in a bind. When doing your own serving, try to remember that most red wine is to be served at room temperature (so don't keep it in the refrigerator between servings) while whites are usually slightly chilled to cold.

RED WINES

Cabernet sauvignon (cab-er-nay saw-ven-yone): A bold, medium to full-bodied wine. Body is predominantly deep, dark fruits, with black currant, cherry, and blackberry most prevalent. Usually aged in oak for a year or more. Primary producers are France, California, Washington state, and Australia.

Merlot (mer-low): A ruby-red, medium to full-bodied wine. Merlot has flavors of cherry and plum, even gooseberry. Less intense than cabernet, with which it is sometimes blended. Primary producers are France, California, Chile, and New Zealand.

Shiraz (shear-ahs), also known as Syrah (sear-ah): A deep dark Australian wine (the original Syrah is from France). Full-bodied and intense with flavors of chocolate, spice, and blackberries.

Zinfandel (zin-fen-dell): A robust ruby-red wine from Italy and California. Highlights include pepper and berry flavors. Not to be confused with white zinfandel, which is a chick wine.

Pinot noir (pea-no no-are): A rich, dark wine. Very fruity, with intricate flavors including black cherries, black currant, red berries, and spicy undertones. Produced in Oregon and France.

Chianti (key-on-tee): A deep, dark wine from the Chianti region of Italy. A clean flavor with hints of black pepper and cherry and a fruity aroma. A popular table wine (meaning you can drink it with almost any meal anytime—cheaply) served room temperature or cold.

WHITE WINES

Chardonnay (shar-duh-nay): An extremely popular dry white wine. Pale yellow to almost honey in color. Medium-bodied, dry wine with hints of peach, honey, figs, cut grass, and butter. California chardonnay is stored in oak, which adds additional flavors. This wine goes with almost anything, especially seafood and lighter dishes.

Sauvignon blanc (sohv-en-yone blahnk): A light to medium-bodied wine. An earthy flavor, with traces of herbs, mint, and either grass or citrus. It used to be the big white wine until chardonnay came along, but is still a popular summer wine. Primary producers are France and New Zealand.

Riesling (reez-ling): A delicate wine with a slight tartness. Mild spice, fruit, and lime flavors. Ranges from very sweet to dry, and is produced in South Africa, France, and Germany.

Gewürztraminer (ga-wer-stra-mean-er): A soft, spicy wine produced in Alsace (France), California, and Washington state. Aroma includes cloves and roses. Light enough for summer drinking, strong enough to go with spicy foods.

Pinot grigio (pee-no gree-zhee-oh), also Pinot gris (pee-no gree): A clean, crisp, refreshing wine. Dry and light-bodied, with hints of honey, melon, and herbs. Grown in Italy, California, and Oregon.

ROSÉ OR BLUSH WINES

These are white or pink wines made from red grapes. Light and usually way too sweet, they are popular with high school kids and college girls. Best avoided.

CHAMPAGNES

Technically and legally, champagnes only come from the Champagne region of France. Any other "champagnes," such as those from California, are accurately defined as sparkling wines and usually state they are produced by the "method champenoise." The best of all of these come from France and California.

WINE TERMS

Aftertaste: the taste that lingers after you've swallowed the wine

Aroma: the grape smell of wine

Balance: proportions of acidity, tannin, and fruit flavor

Body: lightness or heaviness of wine in the mouth. Light, medium, or full.

Bouquet: how the entire wine smells (also called the "nose"). Comes after the aroma.

Breathing: letting the wine come into contact with air

Complexity: different elements of wine tasted over time

Legs: lines of wine adhering to and running down the inside of a glass

Texture: smooth or rough

Odors and flavors detected in wine:

Fruity: black currant, cherry, berries, tropical fruit (melon, pineapple), tree fruit (apple, peach)

Vegetative: green pepper, cut grass, asparagus, olive

Nutty: almond, hazelnut

Woody: vanilla, oak, cedar

Spicy: black pepper, cloves

Caramelized: butter, chocolate, butterscotch, coffee

Floral: rose, violet, orange blossom

SPEED RECORDS

AUTOMOBILE

In October 1997, Andy Green drove his ThrustSSC vehicle to Mach 1.02, averaging 763 mph.

MOTORCYCLE

Donald Vesco drove his Turbinator motorcycle 458 mph in October 2000. By the way, Vesco was sixty-two.

BOAT

In October 1978, Ken Warby drove his jet boat at a speed of 317 mph.

PLANE

In October 1967, Air Force Major William J. "Pete" Knight flew a modified X-15 to a speed of 4,520 mph (Mach 6.7) at an altitude of 102,100 feet.

Mach speed, at ground level is approximately 761.18 mph.

KNOTS, KILOMETERS, AND MILES

A knot is a nautical mile.

One mile equals 1.609344 km or 0.868976 nautical miles.
One mile is 5280 feet.

One kilometer equals 0.62137 of a mile or 0.53996 nautical miles.
One kilometer is 3280.84 feet.

One nautical mile equals 1.852 km or 1.15078 miles.
One nautical mile is 6076.115 feet.

Quick conversion:
6 miles to every 10 kilometers.
11.5 miles to every 10 knots.

MAJOR CRIMES AND THEIR DEFINITIONS

ASSAULT

An assault is an attempt or threat to do physical injury to another. A beating is not necessarily part of assault.

BATTERY

Battery is an actual beating. Assault and battery is threatening to kick the shit out of someone, then doing it.

BURGLARY

Burglary is the unlawful entering of a premises to commit a crime, usually theft. Unlike robbery, burglary does not involve the use of force against another person and the other person need not be present. That means you can burgle someone without them being around. No physical breaking and entering is required in a burglary, you can go right in through an open door.

BREAKING AND ENTERING

Almost the same as burglary, but the act of getting into the place is a crime itself. The breaking means that you didn't just walk in the front door—you forced your way in.

LARCENY

Larceny is the theft or attempted theft of property or cash without using force or illegal entry. This includes pickpocketing, robbing the company cash drawer, shoplifting, stealing bikes from kids in a park, etc.

ROBBERY

Robbery is the felonious and forcible taking of the property of another, against his will, by violence or by putting him in fear. In a robbery, it's up close and personal: the property is taken from the other's person by force, threats, or intimidation. Think bank robbery.

THEFT

Theft is a catchall term for stealing, involving the unlawful taking of another's property with the intent of permanently depriving the owner of the property. It also includes obtaining property, money, or labor through fraud. Theft offenses include burglary, shoplifting, petty theft, grand theft, joyriding, embezzlement, extortion, identity theft, robbery, and fraud.

MURDER

First-degree murder is usually defined as an unlawful killing that is both willful and premeditated, meaning that it was planned and then committed. Suppose you've decided that your religious beliefs won't let you divorce your wife, so you decide to kill her. You plan on putting her in a wood chipper and then mulching your lawn with her. Once you've planned it and done it, you're on the hook for first-degree.

Second-degree murder is usually: 1) an intentional killing that is not premeditated or planned, nor committed in a reasonable "heat of passion," or 2) a killing caused by dangerous conduct and the offender's obvious lack of concern for human life. Such as, you've got a wood chipper in the yard, it's churning away, and you decide that right now would be a good time to toss your wife into it.

Voluntary manslaughter is an intentional killing in which the offender had no prior intent to kill, such as a killing that occurs in the "heat of the moment" or the "heat of passion." The circumstances leading to the killing are the sort that would cause a reasonable person to become emotionally or mentally disturbed. Such as finding your wife in bed with your dad.

Involuntary manslaughter is an unintentional killing that results from recklessness or criminal negligence. Also called "criminally negligent homicide," it is generally regarded as a crime in which the victim's death is unintended. Such as finding your wife in bed with your dad, going out and getting drunk, then accidentally running over and killing your best friend.

• •

DESCRIBING A DUMBSHIT

A few fries short of a Happy Meal.
Elevator doesn't go all the way to the top floor.
Not the sharpest tool in the shed.
The lights are on, but nobody's home.
As sharp as a marble.
A few clowns short of a circus.
Not the brightest bulb on the Christmas tree.
I wish I had a blueprint for his brain; I'm trying to build
   an idiot.
An experiment in Artificial Stupidity.
He only has one oar in the water.
A few beers short of a six-pack.
Dumber than a box of hair.
Dumber than a picnic bench.
Dumber than a box of rocks.

A few peas short of a casserole.

Doesn't have all her Cornflakes in one box.

One Fruit Loop shy of a full bowl.

One taco short of a combination plate.

A few feathers short of a whole duck.

All foam, no beer.

T-shirt that says I'M WITH STUPID and no arrow.

The cheese slid off her cracker.

Body by Fisher, brains by Mattel.

Takes him an hour and a half to watch *60 Minutes*.

If life were an IQ test, he would be dead by now.

Fell out of the stupid tree and hit every branch on the way down.

An intellect rivaled only by garden tools.

As smart as bait.

Chimney's clogged.

Doesn't have all his dogs on one leash.

Forgot to pay her brain bill.

Her sewing machine's out of thread.

His antenna doesn't pick up all the channels.

His belt doesn't go through all the loops.

If she had another brain, it would be lonely.

Missing a few buttons on his remote control.

No grain in the silo.

Proof that evolution can go in reverse.

Receiver is off the hook.

Several nuts short of a full pouch.

Skylight leaks a little.

Slinky's kinked.

Surfing in Nebraska.

Too much yardage between the goalposts.

Not the sharpest knife in the drawer.

Twenty-four cents short of a quarter.

The wheel is spinning, but the hamster's dead.

Got into the gene pool while the lifeguard wasn't watching.

Has an IQ of 2, but it takes 3 to grunt.

Warning: Objects in mirror are dumber than they appear.

Couldn't pour water out of a boot with instructions on the heel.

A room-temperature IQ.

Bright as Alaska in December.

The gates are down, the lights are flashing, but the train isn't coming.

If he were any stupider, he'd have to be watered twice a week.

Some drink from the fountain of knowledge; he just gargled.

Sign in driveway that says CAUTION: SLOW CHILDREN AHEAD.

• •

MANNED MERCURY, GEMINI, AND APOLLO MISSIONS

Mercury was a single-astronaut craft, Gemini housed two, and Apollo carried three.

1961
Mercury 3 • Mercury 4

1962
Mercury 6 • Mercury 7 • Mercury 8

1963
Mercury 9

1965
Gemini 3 • Gemini 4 • Gemini 5 • Gemini 7 • Gemini 6

1966
Gemini 8 • Gemini 9 • Gemini 10 • Gemini 11 • Gemini 12

1968
Apollo 7 • Apollo 8

1969
Apollo 9 • Apollo 10 • Apollo 11 • Apollo 12

1970
Apollo 13

1971
Apollo 14 • Apollo 15

1972
Apollo 16 • Apollo 17

THE TWELVE MEN WHO WALKED ON THE MOON

Neil Armstrong, Apollo 11	1969
Edwin "Buzz" Aldrin, Apollo 11	1969
Charles "Pete" Conrad, Apollo 12	1969
Alan Bean, Apollo 12	1969
Alan Shepard, Apollo 14	1971
Edgar Mitchell, Apollo 14	1971
David Scott, Apollo 15	1971
James Irwin, Apollo 15	1971
John Young, Apollo 16	1972
Charles Duke, Apollo 16	1972
Gene Cernan, Apollo 17	1972
Harrison Schmitt, Apollo 17	1972

DEADLIEST SNAKES

Taipan (Australia)
Black mamba (Africa)
Carpet viper (Asia)
Common krait (Asia)
Australian brown snake (Australia)
Russell's viper (Asia)
Egyptian cobra (Africa)
Sea snake (Pacific and Indian Oceans)
Diamondback rattlesnake (North America)
Boomslang (Africa)

THE ALLIGATOR JOKE, PART 1

A guy enters a bar carrying an alligator and says to the patrons, "Here's a deal. I'll open this alligator's mouth and place my genitals inside. The gator will close his mouth for one minute, then open it, and I'll remove my unit unscathed. If it works, everyone buys me drinks." The crowd agrees. The guy drops his pants and puts his dick in the gator's mouth. The alligator clamps down on the dick—very gently. After a minute, the guy grabs a beer bottle and whacks the gator upside the head. The gator suddenly opens wide, and the guy removes his dick, which is unharmed. Everyone buys him drinks. Then he says: "I'll pay $100 to anyone who's willing to give it a try." After a while, a hand goes up in the back of the bar. It's a woman. "I'll give it a try," she says, "but you have to promise not to hit me on the head with the beer bottle."

THE ALLIGATOR JOKE, PART 2

A guy enters a bar carrying an alligator and says to the patrons, "Here's a deal. I'll open this alligator's mouth and place my genitals inside. The gator will keep his mouth open for ten minutes, and not once will he nip my dick. If it works, everyone buys me drinks." The crowd agrees. The guy drops his pants and puts his dick in the gator's mouth. The gator keeps his mouth open for ten minutes, at which point the guy pulls his dick out. The gator snaps his jaws shut with bone-crushing fury. Everyone buys him drinks. Then he turns to the guy standing next to him. "Hey, you want to give it a try?" he asks. The second guy looks at him and says, "No, thanks. I don't think I could keep my mouth open that long."

SEVEN DEADLY SINS

Greed
Gluttony
Lust
Envy
Sloth
Wrath
Pride

THE FASTEST WAY TO STOP AN ASSAILANT

Let's suppose someone wants to kill you. Face to face. Maybe you accidentally got a BJ from his mom, or you owe him a large gambling debt, or perhaps it's just a crazed assassin with free time on his hands. This person is determined that you will die, and you should be just as determined to live. Unfortunately, you left your machete at home and there are no broken bottles lying around. It's mano a mano. Never fear: here are six essential ways to defend yourself.

1. Jab your thumbs into his eyes, deep. According to military studies, even Marines find it hard to do this without getting a little queasy. But there is no faster way to stop an assailant than to render him blind and in searing pain. The best way to gouge eyeballs is to clap your hands on both sides of his head (as if you were holding a basketball with two hands), bring your thumbs around to where the eyes are nearest the nose, and shove your thumbs in hard. In addition to smashing the eyeball, you can also try wedging your thumbs in between the eyeball and the eye socket and try to dislodge the entire eye from the skull.

2. Rip his ears off. Grotesque, yes, but highly effective, and it requires very little strength. Grab the large flap of the assailant's ear with your hand, then pull quickly toward you and down. The movement is similar to that of pulling a slot machine handle. Since this is an unexpected maneuver in most fights, it may take a moment for the assailant to understand what has just happened. That's when you produce the coup de grâce: hold the ear in your open palm, show it to his face, and then fling it away.

3. Kick his vitals. Like most guys, you were probably told as a child that kicking was for girls. Well, guess

what? The most aggressive ultimate fighting champs kick like rabid mules on meth. Side kicks are most effective, as they leverage your body weight into the blow. If you have to use a front kick, don't use the point of your shoe, boot, or foot. Pretend like you're kicking a door down and go in with the force of your leg driving the flat part of your foot forward. Primary targets should be testicles, knees, stomach, and solar plexus (just under the breastbone).

4. Crush his nose. Punching at your assailant's head during a fight is dicey. You risk breaking bones in your fingers and hands if you land a misplaced blow on the thickest areas of the skull or the jaw. However, if you can jam his nose straight back into his head—using either the butt of your palm with fingers curled up or a fist—you are likely to shut him down fast. The resultant blood spray and watery tears will render him virtually blind. Unless you shoved nose cartilage into his brain. Then he might be dead.

5. Elbow to his chin. A good bone-jarring uppercut where your elbow slams his lower jaw into his upper jaw may actually knock your assailant out. This can be done by either swinging your elbow up and in to hit his chin with the broad side of your arm and el-bow, or forcing it away and across using the point of your elbow.

6. Karate chop to his throat. Even if you don't know karate, this can actually be lethal, which of course

may be what you're looking for. Chop right into his Adam's apple with a sideswipe. It doesn't take much to cause choking and gagging. With more ferocity, it can crush a windpipe and prevent any further breathing.

Tips: Don't punch bone and thick muscle. It does minimal damage when you strike someone in the chest or the arms and you can hurt your hands in the process. Aim for soft, unprotected tissue. If you are punching, the stomach, groin, throat, and solar plexus are your best bets for dropping an assailant.

There's something else you should know: Many of these moves are designed to kick your assailant's ass so bad that he ends up in the hospital . . . or in the morgue. Conversely, that means you could end up in jail . . . or on death row. That's because the use of lethal force is frowned on by local law-enforcement agencies everywhere, not to mention prosecuting attorneys. For that reason, we don't recommend that you attempt to take out some moron who's bugging you at a bar or the idiot who's rooting too loud for the other team at the stadium. You should only apply deadly force when your own life—or that of a loved one, like the hot babe you just met who has given you every indication that she's ready to jump into your bed after one more drink—is in imminent danger.

IMPORTANT GOLF TERMS

Back lip: the edge of a bunker that is farthest from the hole.

Back nine: the second nine holes on an eighteen-hole course.

Birdie: one stroke under par on a hole.

Bogey: a score of one over the designated par for a hole. As a verb, to score a bogey. Also spelled "bogie."

Bye: in match-play tournaments, a free pass to the next round without having to compete.

Chip-and-run: a chip shot, usually hit from just off the green, on which the ball rolls a considerable distance toward the hole after landing.

Chip shot: a short approach shot with a low trajectory, usually hit with topspin or backspin.

Condor: a triple eagle, that is, four under par on a hole. A very rare occurrence, since it requires a hole in one on a par 5 hole.

Dead ball: a ball that is so close to the hole that there's no doubt it will be sunk with the next putt.

Deuce: a hole made in two strokes.

Dogleg: a bend in the fairway.

Double bogey: a score of two over the designated par for a hole.

Double eagle: a score of three under the designated par for a hole.

Down: the number of holes, in match play, or the number of strokes, in stroke play, that a player is behind an opponent.

Eagle: two strokes under the designated par for a hole. Also used as a verb, as in, "He eagled the ninth hole."

Fade: a controlled shot on which the ball curves slightly from left to right at the end of its flight, when hit by a right-handed golfer. As a verb, to hit such a shot.

Fan: to swing and miss the ball completely.

Gimme: an easy putt that is likely to be conceded by the opponent.

Handicap: the number of strokes deducted from a player's gross score to determine the net score. It's essentially based on the player's average score over a period of time, minus par.

Handicap player: a player whose average score is above par, and who therefore is given a handicap in certain kinds of competition.

Hanging lie: a lie in which the ball rests on a downhill slope.

Hook: a shot that curves from right to left for a right-handed golfer.

Lay up: to hit a shot that will stop short of a hazard, rather than risking the hazard by attempting a longer shot to the green.

Leader board: a sign on which the scores of the leading golfers are posted during a tournament.

Lie: the position of the ball after it comes to rest anywhere between the tee and the putting surface. A lie is described as good if the ball can be struck cleanly.

Long game: that part of the game of golf involving shots in which distance is important.

Mulligan: in casual play, a golfer who hits a poor tee

shot is sometimes allowed to take a second shot without penalty. The second shot is called a "mulligan." It's usually allowed only on the first tee.

Par: the number of strokes, designated for each hole, that represents a standard of good performance. The par figures for individual holes are added up to represent par for a course. Par is generally based on the length of a hole from the tee to the green, although adjustments may be made for configuration of the ground, severity of hazards, and other difficult or unusual conditions.

Penalty stroke: an additional stroke that's added to a player's score because of a rules violation.

Read the green: to examine the slope and texture of the green in order to determine what path the ball should take on a putt.

Rough: areas of long grass adjacent to the teeing ground, fairway, greens, or hazards.

Scratch golfer: a player has a zero handicap; thus, one who averages par.

Shank: to hit a shot with the shank, which causes it to go sharply off line, usually to the right for a right-handed golfer.

Skins: a betting game in which the player who wins a hole wins a pot. If there is no winner, the pot is carried over and added to the pot for the next hole.

Slice: a shot that curves strongly from left to right, for a right-handed golfer, because of clockwise rotation. As a verb, to hit such a shot.

Stroke: a swing at the ball with the intent of hitting it. A golfer's swing.

Triple bogey: a score of three over the designated par for a hole.

Unplayable lie: a lie from which it's impossible to play the ball, such as when it's wedged between two rocks. The player is allowed to drop the ball, incurring a one-stroke penalty.

Wormburner: a hard hit ball that stays close to the ground.

Yips: a severe case of nerves resulting in convulsive shakes that make it difficult for a player to putt accurately.

PAR MEASUREMENTS

Par 3 hole. Up to 250 yards in length for men, 210 yards for women.

Par 4 hole. 250 to 471 yards in length for men, 211 to 400 yards for women.

Par 5 hole. More than 470 yards in length for men, more than 401 yards for women.

THE GREATEST GOLFERS OF ALL TIME

Odds are that at some point in your life you will play golf. You will either embrace it like a new girlfriend or reject it like a crab-laden hooker. For those of us who choose to embrace it, golf is a game rich in history, style, frustration, and sheer joy. All golfers harbor a hidden desire to play in a ProAm before the end of their lives, and perhaps rub shoulders—if only for a moment—with the true greats of the game.

The following men are golf's icons: they were so great that they changed the nature of the game. Their techniques should be studied and revered by every golfer who ever wants to make par.

Jack Nicklaus

Ben Hogan

Sam Snead

Tiger Woods

Robert Jones

Byron Nelson

Arnold Palmer

Walter Hagen

Gary Player

Tom Watson

Gene Sarazen

Harry Vardon

Lee Trevino

Billy Casper

Nick Faldo

GOLF AND SEX

A man playing golf slices into the woods. When he goes to find the ball, he discovers a witch stirring a cauldron. Curious, he asks her what she is brewing.

"A magic golfer's potion," she replies.

The man is skeptical. "What's it for?"

"This potion will make anyone an excellent golfer."

At this the golfer gets really excited and asks if he can have some. She is agreeable but warns him that it could ruin his sex life. Nonetheless, he decides to try the potion. He goes back to the golf course and completes an excellent game of golf. Next he challenges the golf pro and beats him. He spends every possible moment of the next year playing golf and at every course he plays and has a wonderful time of it. After a year he finds himself back at the same course where he found the witch. Out of curiosity he slices one into the woods so he can talk to her.

"Well," she asks, "how has your game been?"

"Great! This has been the best year of my life. I've played every day and never lost a game."

"And how about your sex life?"

"Not too bad," says the man.

"Really? This stuff can destroy a guy's sex life. How many times did you have sex last year?"

"Hmm. I think it was three or four times."

The witch scoffed. "You call that not bad?"

"Not for a priest with a small parish."

HOTTEST ANIMATED WOMEN

CATWOMAN (*BATMAN*)

The whips, the claws, the vinyl bodysuit. Most guys aren't man enough to handle this type of pussy.

JESSICA RABBIT (*WHO FRAMED ROGER RABBIT?*)

No matter what she says, she *is* bad, and she's drawn that way.

DAPHNE (*SCOOBY-DOO*)

The miniskirt, the supermodel hair, and always up for some late-night adventure. Don't you wonder what she does to unwind?

LARA CROFT (*TOMB RAIDER* VIDEO GAME)

34D-24-35, plus handguns. That about sums it up.

AEON FLUX (*AEON FLUX* SERIES)

As unbelievable as it might sound, this leather-thonged assassin is actually hotter than Charlize Theron, who played her in the live-action version. That thought alone is boner-inducing.

MELODY (*JOSIE AND THE PUSSYCATS*)

The dumb blonde behind the drum kit is a good enough reason for guys to become rock and roll groupies.

JUDY JETSON (*THE JETSONS*)

The original sci-fi Girl Gone Wild. You know there's a spring break video of her getting drunk somewhere in the universe.

MARY JANE WATSON-PARKER (*SPIDER-MAN*)

Peter Parker was a geek, but he got this babe. And she is way hotter than Lois Lane.

BETTY RUBBLE (*THE FLINTSTONES*)

The miniskirt, the small waist, the great laugh—she's like Audrey Hepburn made out of crayons. If cave women really looked this way, we'd start believing in intelligent design.

FUJIKO MINE (*LUPIN III*)

This manga babe is a skilled burglar, an expert marksman, and sports a rack that makes Pamela Anderson look like Kate Moss. Fujiko is named after Mt. Fuji, and rumor has it that the English translation of her name is "twin peaks" . . . both of which barely fit into her tight blouse.

LOIS GRIFFIN (*FAMILY GUY*)

For a middle-aged mom, Lois knows how to work it better than most real-life moms. Our candidate for the animated MILF Hall of Fame.

ARIEL (*THE LITTLE MERMAID*)

You have to love a Disney cartoon character whose entire wardrobe is just two seashells that barely cover C-cups. She has some serious lung capacity and we're guessing she can hold her breath pretty much forever. One potential drawback: might be jailbait.

· ·

PICKING UP GIRLS

The most daunting aspect of a man's life is trying to find the right woman, often known as "the little lady," "Mrs. Right," or "the Final Sperm Bank." Over the course of many years, you have to "experience" several females to figure out what you want. But since women don't want to be picked over as part of your selection process, there's going to be some tension. Plus, a woman has to want you as much as you want her, and let's face it, that's not always going to be the case. Especially if your dream girl was just on the cover of the *Sports Illustrated* swimsuit edition.

In the real world, if you see a woman you are interested in, you cannot act like the only thing you're interested in is sex—especially if you are. Spend five minutes going through any women's magazine and you'll find that females look for just four things in men: 1) a guy who makes them feel special, 2) a guy with a good sense of humor, 3) a guy who has a decent job and isn't living with his mom, and 4) someone who bathes and can dress himself up nicely. That's it, four simple things. You've got to be interesting, interested, amusing, and clean.

It's not all about money, so forget that excuse. The richest guy on the planet, Bill Gates, ended up having to marry someone who worked for him because he didn't get high scores on any of the four basic requirements. Celebrity babes are always complaining that no one ever asks them out except for stuck-up rich guys. That means you have a shot with most women—females now out-number males, population-wise, putting the odds in your favor—so don't blow it.

Here are some essential tips for ensuring that you'll at least break the ice and maybe get a little skating time in when you're ready to start looking for that special woman. Or at least tonight's special woman.

1) When approaching a girl for the first time, DO NOT use stupid pickup lines. Ever. They will get you an ex-press ticket back to self-love land. Anything that re-motely resembles the following lame come-ons should be permanently erased from your repertoire.

You have a great set of legs. What time do they open?
My friend and I have a bet that you won't take off your
  blouse in a public place.
Excuse me. Would you like to see something swell?
Are you from Tennessee? Because you're the only ten
  I see.
Screw me if I'm wrong, but haven't we met before?
I just wanted to let you know I've moved you to the top of
  my to-do list.
Didn't I see you on the cover of *Vogue*?
Are you as beautiful on the inside as you are on the out-
  side?
Should I call you in the morning or nudge you?
Did it hurt? When you fell out of heaven?
You're so hot that you melt the plastic in my underwear.

Would you like to come over to my place later? You can
   bring some friends because my face seats five.
My name is Fred Flintstone and I am ready to make your
   Bed rock.
Are you accepting applications for your fan club?
Do you work for UPS? Because I could have sworn I saw
   you checking out my package.
They call me "coffee" because I grind so fine.
Hey babe, want to make an easy fifty bucks?

2) If you've made yourself presentable and done the best
you can with the looks God may or may not have given
you, then start with humor. Women want to laugh and to
know you're interested in them. Or talk about something
near and dear to women's hearts: their shoes and clothes.
Most of all, be yourself and be calm. Try not to stutter or
spit when you speak. Use conversational lines like the
following:

Those are really cool shoes.
Pardon me, that is a great watch. Do you mind if I ask
   what kind it is?
You know, I think you might be asked to leave soon.
   You're making the other women here look really bad.

3) Never tell a woman she reminds you of anything. That
includes your mom, sister, wife, daughter, ex-girlfriend,
the sun, the stars, a garden, a moonlit pool, heaven, a
model, a movie star, or a beautiful day. Any woman who
falls for those lines probably doesn't know the difference
between a penis and a pencil, anyway, and thus doesn't
know how to use either one.

4) If you can engage a girl in conversation as part of a group at a party or a bar, so much the better. You can hear what she talks about and build on that. Most of all, DO NOT talk about yourself until she asks. You need to learn what interests her. Wait until you're in bed to tell her what you're really interested in.

5) Give her some space. Sometimes you have to watch a woman's body language before talking to her. If she's sitting at a bar just drinking, see if she asks the bartender questions. If there's a question you can help with, volunteer the answer without making a big deal out of it. If she's looking around for something/someone repeatedly, ask her if she needs help finding something. NEVER ask it like a panting dog; ask as if you were just giving directions to a stranger. Then see how she replies.

6) Helpful hint: You can tell how hot a girl thinks she is by how pointed her shoes are. It has nothing to do with the heels; it's all in the toes. The pointier the shoe, the sexier she thinks she is. A rounded-toe shoe means there's not a lot of self-confidence there. Use this to your advantage.

If none of these work, you might find yourself thinking, *Maybe I just ought to pay for sex.* An age-old and practical tradition, certainly, but one that might just land you in the local house of detention. Many towns and cities now post the names of johns caught in the act with prostitutes in the local newspaper or on a Web site. Not the kind of publicity anyone wants, even if they spell your name correctly.

Most major cities have escort services listed in the phone book. Escort is an upscale term for a lady who will spend quality time with your genitals for a lot of money. If you're caught having sex with an escort, though, it still counts as prostitution and could result in a fine, a night in jail, and serious humiliation. Especially if the escort keeps your name in one of those "little black books" that seem to make the tabloid news every so often.

If you are committed to buying sex safely, you're probably going to have to buy a plane ticket, and maybe get a passport. In the United States, only Nevada has legal prostitution, and its brothels have a reputation for being clean and friendly places. However, the brothels are few and far between and Nevada covers more than a hundred thousand square miles. On the other hand, countries like the Netherlands, Denmark, Germany, Canada, and New Zealand all have legal and locally accessible houses of ill-repute, often in tourist-friendly red-light districts.

While most countries with legal prostitution regulate their working girls, you're taking your chances if you decide to go to the back alleys found throughout Asia. Dick-eating diseases run rampant in Thailand, Vietnam, China, and other up-and-coming sex service nations. No matter where you decide to get your retail jollies, always bring plenty of condoms, get your shots, and make sure your health insurance is completely paid up.

THE FINEST INSULTS EVER MADE

"A modest little person, with much to be modest about."
—**Winston Churchill**

"In order to avoid being called a flirt, she always yielded easily." —**Charles, Count Talleyrand**

"I didn't attend the funeral, but I sent a nice letter saying I approved of it." —**Mark Twain**

"I've just learned about his illness. Let's hope it's nothing trivial." —**Irvin S. Cobb**

"I have never killed a man, but I have read many obituaries with great pleasure." —**Clarence Darrow**

"I feel so miserable without you, it's almost like having you here." —**Stephen Bishop**

"He is a self-made man and worships his creator."
—**John Bright**

"He has all the virtues I dislike and none of the vices I admire." —**Winston Churchill**

"He has never been known to use a word that might send a reader to the dictionary." —**William Faulkner, about Ernest Hemingway**

"Poor Faulkner. Does he really think big emotions come from big words?" —**Ernest Hemingway, about William Faulkner**

"Thank you for sending me a copy of your book; I'll waste no time reading it." —**Moses Hadas**

"His ears made him look like a taxicab with both doors open."—**Howard Hughes, about Clark Gable**

"He is not only dull himself, he is the cause of dullness in others." —**Samuel Johnson**

"He is simply a shiver looking for a spine to run up." —**Paul Keating**

"He had delusions of adequacy." —**Walter Kerr**

"There's nothing wrong with you that reincarnation won't cure." —**Jack E. Leonard**

"He can compress the most words into the smallest idea of any man I know." —**Abraham Lincoln**

"I've had a perfectly wonderful evening. But this wasn't it." —**Groucho Marx**

"They never open their mouths without subtracting from the sum of human knowledge." —**Thomas Brackett Reed**

"He inherited some good instincts from his Quaker forebears, but by diligent hard work, he overcame them." —**James Reston, about Richard Nixon**

"He loves nature in spite of what it did to him." —**Forrest Tucker**

"Why do you sit there looking like an envelope without any address on it?" —**Mark Twain**

"His mother should have thrown him away and kept the stork." —**Mae West**

"Some cause happiness wherever they go; others whenever they go." —**Oscar Wilde**

"He has no enemies, but is intensely disliked by his friends." —**Oscar Wilde**

"He uses statistics as a drunken man uses lampposts—for support rather than illumination." —**Andrew Lang**

"He has van Gogh's ear for music." —**Billy Wilder**

TENNIS GRAND SLAM WINNERS

The four matches that comprise the tennis "Gram Slams" are Wimbledon, the U.S. Open, the French Open, and the Australian Open.

14   Pete Sampras
12   Roger Federer

12 Roy Emerson
11 Rod Laver
11 Björn Borg
10 Bill Tilden
 9 Ken Rosewall
 8 Andre Agassi
 8 Jimmy Connors
 8 Ivan Lendl
 8 Fred Perry

Rod Laver and Don Budge are the only men to hold all four grand slams at once.

. . . .

THINGS NEVER TO SAY DURING SEX

Do I have to pay for this?
You look better in the dark.
Oh mommy, mommy!
This is much better than my last girlfriend.
You've got to be kidding me.
(phone rings) Hello? Oh nothing, and you?
Do I have to call you tomorrow?
I thought that goes in the other hole . . .
Don't tell my wife.
You have the same bra my mom does.
This sucks.
Can you finish now? I have a meeting . . .
I hope you don't expect a raise for this . . .

I think you might get the job for this.

Damn! Is that all you know how to do?

Did I tell you I have herpes?

Hurry up, the game's about to start.

I'm hungry.

I'm thirsty.

Zzzzzzzzzzz.

Are you trying to be funny?

Can I have a ride home after this?

Are those real?

Is that real?

By the way, I want to break up.

Is that smell coming from you?

Haven't you ever done this before?

Wow!! I've never seen those before (then grope wildly).

You're so much like your sister . . .

Your mom's cute.

What's your name again?

Do I have to be here in the morning?

A second time? I barely stayed awake the first time!

But you just started!

You're about as good as a nine-year-old, and I should know.

Don't touch that!

Can we order a pizza?

I think my mom is listening at the door.

Smile for the camera, honey!

Get your hand off that!

I think the condom broke ten minutes ago.

I knew you wore a padded bra!

Cover me boys, I'm going in!

DIVE! DIVE! DIVE!

Fire one!

God, those are small!

Hold on, let me change the channel . . .

Who smells like fish?

Is it okay if my mom (and/or dad) joins in?

Your best friend does it much better.

I hope you don't mind; I left my boots on.

Hurry up, the motor's running.

You're fogging up the windshield.

Can I borrow five bucks?

What the hell was that noise?!

Stop moaning; you sound so stupid.

Shut up, bitch! (worse if the girl says it)

You know, you're not really attractive.

I'm sorry, I wasn't listening.

What? Oh yeah, I love you too, now let me concentrate!

Stop interrupting me!

I have to take a shit.

Your breath is funky.

Is it okay if I call someone?

It's okay honey, I'll just imagine they're bigger.

God, I wish you were a real woman.

Why can't you ever shave your legs?

By the way, when I drove over here, I ran over your
   dog . . .

Your breast milk is like my mom's . . .

You're hairy.

Your "happy trail" led me to a dead end.

Is it okay if I never see you again?

Did I forget to tell you I got worms from my cat?

Don't make that face at me!

You're boring.
Suck my dick, bitch.
How much do I owe you?
How come we each have a penis?
No, you can't be on top. You're too fat, you'll kill me.
Your ass is hairy.
Just use your hand; it's wetter.
Does your family have to watch?
We'll try again later when you can satisfy me, too.
Get off me, I'll do it myself!
Can you hold this sandwich for me?
You're as soft as a sheep, inside and out.
The only reason I'm doing this is because I'm drunk.
My mom taught me this . . .
How cute . . . peach fuzz.
Damn girl! My tits are bigger than yours!
Should I ask why you're bleeding?
This is my pet rat, Larry . . .
If you can't do it, I'll find someone else who can.
Wanna see me take out my glass eye?
No, I don't love your mind, I can't grab that.
I'm sobering up and you're getting ugly!
You're no better than my sister!
Mooooo!
Fire in the hole!
I want to see how many quarters I can fit in there.
Hurry up, I'm late for a date.
I'm out of condoms. Can I use a sock?
Don't squirm, you'll spill my beer.
Did I tell you where my cold sore came from?
I think I just shit on your bed.
Of course I don't love you.

You wanted me to use a condom?
Is it okay if I tell my friends about this?
Oh Susan, Susan . . . I mean Donna . . .

• •

THE HARDEST THINGS TO DO IN SPORTS

Ride in the Tour de France
Hit a baseball thrown at 90 mph
Stop a slap shot from the blue line
Drive a race car in excess of 120 mph around a crowded
   track
Pole vault heights of over 15 feet
Return a 120 mph tennis serve
Stop a soccer penalty kick
Ski downhill faster than 80 mph
Run a marathon
Hit a golf ball long and straight
Land a quad in figure skating

• •

TOP TEN CAUSES OF DEATH IN MEN

1) Diseases of the heart   29.3%
2) Malignant neoplasms (cancer)   24.3%
3) Cerebrovascular diseases (stroke)   5.5%

4) Accidents (unintentional injuries)   5.4%
5) Chronic lower respiratory diseases   5.1%
6) Diabetes mellitus   2.7%
7) Influenza and pneumonia   2.4%
8) Intentional self-harm (suicide)   2.0%
9) Nephritis, nephrotic syndrome, and
   nephrosis (kidney disease)   1.5%
10) Chronic liver disease and cirrhosis   1.5%

Not surprisingly, each of these (with the exception of accidents and suicides) can be treated if detected early on. We know it bites going to the doctor. But do it anyway. At least once every ten years.

• •

THE MOST DARING FEATS EVER DONE BY GUYS

BREAKING THE SOUND BARRIER
Chuck Yeager
October 14, 1947

Flying an experimental jet that was little more than a missile with a seat, Chuck Yeager was the first person to fly faster than the speed of sound. He took his X-1 to Mach 1.06—about 662 mph. Although the plane shook violently, no one had ever tested a plane at that speed. Yeager rode it out for twenty seconds before decelerating.

ASCENT OF MT. EVEREST
Sir Edmund Hillary and Tenzing Norgay
March 29, 1953

Hillary and Norgay made it to the top of the world without GPS, cell phones, aluminum ladders, or carved trails. Just two guys climbing straight up more than 29,000 feet. Since then, approximately two thousand people have reached the summit, and more than two hundred have died trying.

VOYAGE TO THE BOTTOM OF THE SEA
Jacques Piccard and Don Walsh
January 23, 1960

These two rode the submersible *Trieste* to the bottom of the Marianas Trench in the Pacific Ocean. It set a deep-sea diving record that still stands: 35,810 feet, about seven miles, which is deeper than Mt. Everest is high. The water pressure at that depth is more than eight tons per square inch.

FREE-FALLING TO EARTH
Joseph Kittinger
August 16, 1960

Air Force Captain Kittinger jumped from a helium balloon at a height of 102,800 feet, nearly nineteen miles up. For reference, jet airliners fly at six miles up. In free-fall for almost five minutes, Kittinger reached 614 mph, and finally pulled his parachute at 18,000 feet. The temperature during the drop was -94°F and it took Kittinger thirteen minutes and forty-five seconds to reach the ground. Five decades later, his record has still never been matched.

AROUND THE WORLD ALONE IN A BOAT
Sir Francis Chichester
May 28, 1967

One man, one boat, nine months. 28,500 miles. All around the world.

WALKING ON THE MOON
Neil Armstrong
July 29, 1969

Getting out of that hatch and putting his foot on the moon was one of mankind's greatest achievements. Before Armstrong got there, no one knew how it would turn out. It could have been a bad science-fiction movie, complete with nasty results. But it wasn't. And Armstrong came home.

TIGHTROPE WALKING BETWEEN THE WORLD TRADE CENTER TOWERS
Philipe Petit
August 14, 1974

Petit walked one thousand feet above Manhattan on a thin wire—without a net. He walked between the towers eight times, and lay down on it. Most guys wouldn't lean over the edge of a tall building for a billion dollars; Petit walked off one for the thrill of it.

A LAWN CHAIR OVER LAX
Larry Walters
July 2, 1982

In his Los Angeles backyard, Larry strapped himself into a lawn chair equipped with forty-two helium weather balloons. He had a pellet gun, some soda, and a parachute. He expected to float over his neighbors' homes and out toward the desert. He'd shoot the balloons when he was ready to come down. Instead, he shot up to 16,000 feet. Too nervous to shoot his balloons at that height, his lawn chair flew into commercial aircraft space. His lawn chair was reported by TWA and Delta airlines pilots before he floated to earth—into some power lines—about an hour later.

• •

1000 WORDS FOR FEMALE GENITALIA

A

ace • ace of spades • agreeable ruts of life • alimony alley • all pink on the inside • alley • altar of love • altar of hymen • altar of pleasure • aperture of bliss • apparatus • apparatus urogenitalis • arsenal • artichoke • article • Aunt Annie • Aunt Maria • Aunt Mary • axe wound

B

baby chute • baby factory • baby in the boat • bacon bomb doors • bacon hole • bacon sandwich • badger •

bag of tricks • bald man in a boat • ball jar • banger hanger • bank • barge • basket • basket of goodies • bawdy cleft • bayonet wound • bazoo • bear trapper's hat • beard • beard flit • bearded • bearded clam • bearded lady • bearded leisure center • bearded oyster • bearded taco • bearskin • beauty spot • beaver • beaver tail • beaver trap • The Beave • beehive • beef box • beef curtains • beef flaps • beetle bonnet • belly bristles • belly entrance • belly thicket • belly whiskers • below the navel • Bermuda Triangle • big V • bilabial trump card • bird's nest • birthplace • bit • bit of fish • bit o' flesh • bit of jam • bit of pork • black box • black hole • blind alley • blind entrance • blind eye • blivvet • blood bank • blood flaps • blood box • bloody axe gash • bloomer pudding • Bluebeard's closet • blurt • boat • bottomless pit • bovine drapes • box • box with teeth • boy in the boat • boy hole • brakes • breadbasket • bread factory • breakfast of champions • briar patch • Brillo pad • brush • bubblicious • bucket • bull ring • bull's eye • bum bacon • bunghole • bush • bush garden • bush pie • butcher's shop • butcher's window • butter boat • butter box • butterfly • buttonhole

C

cabbage • cabbage field • cabbage garden • cabbage patch • cake • camel toe • can • canyon • Cape of Good Hope • Cape Horn • carnal parts • carnal trap • carpet • cat • cave • cave of harmony • cavern • cellar • center of attraction • center of bliss • center of joy • central office • chamber of Venus • cheesecake • cheese factory • cherry blossom • cherry pit • cherry pudding • chicko •

chimney • choot • cum hole • chow box • chuff • chuff box • chum • churn • circulus vitiosus • civet • clam • claptrap • cleft • Clint Toris • clit • clitty • cloven inlet • cloven spot • clover field • cloven stamp of female distinction • coal scuttle • cock alley • cock chafer • cock hall • cock holder • cock hotel • Cock Inn • Cock Lane • cock loft • cockles • cockpit • cock wash • cod cove • coffee grinder • coin slot • columns of Venus • contrapunctum • controlling part • cooch • cookie • cookies • coot • cooter • cootchie • cooze • cotton • covered way • crack • crack of heaven • cradle • cranny • cream catcher • cream jug • crease • crevice • crotch • crotch crater • cuckoo's nest • cud • cunny • cunny skin • cunny warren • cunt • cunt carpet • cunt curtain • cunt down • cunt hair • cunt lips • cuntikin • cunt pie • cuntlet • cuntocks • Cupid's alley • Cupid's cave • Cupid's cloister • Cupid's cupboard • Cupid's hotel • curlies • curly hairs • curtains • cush • cushion • cut • cuzzie • c-word • cylinder

D

daisy • damp • dangly bits • dark • dark hole • dark paradise • dead end street • dearest bodily part • The Deep • delicate glutton • delta • devilish thing • dew flaps • dickey dido • dick wallet • dickweed • dike • Dilberry brush • dimple • ditch • divine scar • divine monosyllable • docking bay • dog's mouth • doodle-case • double doors • donut • down • down below • down south • down there • downy cave • drain • dugout • dumb glutton • dumb oracle • dumb squint

E

ear-between-the-legs • Eden hole • empty tunnel • end of the sentimental journey • engine • Everglades • Eve's custom house • evening socket • everlasting wound • eye that weeps most when best pleased

F

fascinating fur piece • fat rabbit • female cock • female coital apparatus • female funnel • female gewgaw • female genital appeaser • female goodies • female hiatus • female inlet • female interlabial oven • female-lipped underbelly • female lower mouth • female netherland • female organ of generation • female perineal cul-de-sac • female phallus • female pudendal canal • female pudendal chamber • female pudendalia • female pudendum • female sex • female slit • female underbelly • female vulvar apparatus • female's lower kisser • fern • fillet o' fish • finger pie • fireplace • fires of hell • fish box • fish hole • fish lips • fish market • fish mitten • fish taco • flabby lips • flange • flaps • flat tail • fleece • flesh beer towels • flesh wallet • flounder • flower • fly cage • flycatcher • flytrap • fool trap • forecastle • forest • fornicators hall • Fort Bushy • fount of femininity • foyer • fresh axe wound in a bear's back • frizzle • front anus • front attic • front bum • front door • front door-mat • front doors • front entrance • front garden • front parlor • front passage • front porch • front room • front window • fruitful vine • fuck flaps • fuck fur • fuck hatch • fuck hole • fumbler's hall • fun hole • fun zone • funk hole • fur • fur below • fur burger • fur chalice • fur forest • fur pie • furrow • furry bicycle stand • furry bush • furry hoop • furry letterbox • furry mongoose • furry mound • furze • furze bush • futz • fuzz • fuzz box • fuzz burger • fuzzies • fuzzy bunny • fuzzy cup • fuzzy-muzzy • fuzzy wuzzles

G

gap • gap over the garter • gaper • garage • garden • garden gates • garden hedge • garden of Eden • gash • genital chamber • genital smile • genitalia • gentle trap • gentleman's delight • gentleman's garden • geography • gimcrack • girl beard • glory hole • glue pot • gnat meat • goalkeeper • goat milker • goatee • gold mine • golden donut • golden gate • golden mound • good parts • gooseberry bush • gorge • gorilla burger • Grand Canyon • gravy giver • gravy maker • grease box • Great Divide • greedy pussy lips • green grove • green meadow • grin • gristle-gripper • groin • grotto • Grove of Eglantine • growl • gully • gully hole • gut entrance • gutter • gym • gymnasium

H

hair burger • hair court • hair pie • hairy axe wound • hairy cup • hairy donut • hairy lasso • hairy magnet • hairy oracle • hairy pie • hairy ring • Hairy Mary • happy hunting grounds • happy valley • harbor of hope • hatch • heater • heaven • heaven's porthole • hefty clefty • hell • hey-nonny-no • hidden fortress • hidden treasure • hirsute oyster • ho cake • hog eye • hole • hole of content • hole of holes • hole to hide it in • Holiday Inn • holiest of holies • Holy Grail • home sweet home • honey pie • honey pot • hoochie • hoochie koo •

hoo-hoo • hoop • horse collar • hot box • hot spot •
house under the hill • husband's supper • hypogastrian
cranny • hymeneal waterfall

I

Inglenook • inland passage • inlet • inner lips • inner
sanctum • inner self • interlabial hiatus • interlabial
sanctum • intimate bits • intimate parts • Irish pasture •
it • itchy place • ivory gate

J

jade gates • jam • jam donut • jam pot • Janey • jelly
bag • jelly box • jelly cave • jelly jar • jellyroll • Jerusalem
artichoke • jewel case • jewelry • jimcrack • jing-jang •
jinny • joy box • joy buzzer • joy furrow • joy hole • joy
trail • juicy sewer • junioress

K

kennel • ketchup dispenser • kettle • keyhole • kitchen •
kitten's ear • kitty • kitty kat • knickknack • knish

L

la belle chose • labia lips • ladder • ladies' treasure • lady flower • Lady Jane • lady star • lady's low
toupee • lady's welcome mat • lamp of love • Lapland •
lawn • leg beard • life's dainty • ling • lipped pudendal
entree • lipped underside • lips • little boy in the boat •
little bud • little kitten • little man in the boat • little
Mary • little monkey • little shame tongue • little sister •
living fountain • lobster pot • lodge • loins • Lord

knows what • Lord knows where • lotus • love box • love bucket • love bud • love button • love canal • love chamber • love cleft • love crater • love flesh • love glove • love grotto • love lane • love nest • love organ • love pouch • love sheath • love tunnel • love's harbor • love's paradise • love's pavilion • lovely flower • lover's lane • low countries • lower lips • lower mouth • lower wig • lowlands • lucky bag • lunch box

M

Madge • magnet • magic muscle • magic monkey • main avenue • male catcher • mama's box • man catcher • man eater • man entrapment • man hole • man in the boat • man trap • mangle • manometer • marble arch • mark of the beast • masterpiece • mat • maw • meat • meat curtains • meat tarp • melting pot • merkin • middle cut • middle eye • middle kingdom • midlands • milk can • milk jug • milk pan • milker • milking pail • mine of pleasure • minge • Miss Kitty • moist muffin • moist oyster • mole catcher • Molly's hole • Mom's best friend • money • money box • moneymaker • money pot • monkey • monosyllable • mortar • moss • moss rose • mossy bank • mossy cell • mossy doughnut • mossy face • mossy mound • mot • mother of all saints • mother of all souls • mound • Mount Joy • Mount Pleasant • mouse hole • mousetrap • mouser • mouth of nature • mouth that cannot bite • mouth that says no words • moving parts • mowed lawn • much-traveled highway • mud flaps • muff • muff pie • muffet • muffin • mustard and cress • mustard pot • mute mouth • mutton • mystic grotto

N

naf • naggy • name-it-not • nameless • nanny • nappy • nappy dugout • nasty • natural parts • natural places • naturals • nature's veil • naughty • naughty bits • naval base • naviculans • necessaries • needle book • needle case • nest in the bush • nether end • nether eye • nether eyebrow • nether lashes • nether whiskers • nether lips • nether mouth • nether parts • nether regions • netherland sanctum • Netherlands • niche • nick • nick-nack • nick in the notch • night depository • nock • nonesuch • nonny-no • nonny-nonny • nonesuch • nook • nooker • nookie • nooky • noony • noose • notch • nothing • novelty • nub • nubbin • Number Nip • nursery

O

oat bin • old frizzle • one that bites • open C • open charms • open well • open wound • opening • oracle • orchard of the Hesperides • organ • organ grinder • organ of reproduction • organs of generation • orgasm chasm • orgasm hole • outer lips • oven • ox drapes • oyster • oyster catcher

P

P-maker • package • padded box • padlock • palace gates • palace of pleasure • pan • pancake • Pandora's box • panty pudding • papaya • parlor • parlor room • parsley bed • parsley patch • parts below • parts of generation • parts of shame • passion flaps • passion hole • passion pit • patch • peach-fish • peculiar river • pee hole •

pee-pee hole • peeping sentinel • pencil sharpener •
penis equivalent • penis femininis • penis flytrap • perineal genital mouth • periwinkle • phallic haven • pie •
pillcock hill • pillicock hill • pink • pink bits • pink dick
wallet • petals • pink eye • pink flaps • pink palace in
the black forest • pink pearl • pink surprise • pink
tortellini • pink velvet sausage wallet • pinkwing • pipe •
pipkin • piss flaps • piss slit • pisser • pit • pit hole • pit
mouth • pit of darkness • pitcher • pitchka • placket •
placket box • playing field • playpen • plaything • pleas-
urable underside • pleasure boat • pleasure garden •
pleasure ground • pleasure place • plush • pocketbook •
poke hole • pole hole • pole vault • pond • poon • poon-
tang • poontenanny • poor man's blessing • poota •
pooz • poozie • poozle • porcupine • portal of love • portal of Venus • portals of sex • porthole • pot of gold •
pouch • pouter • praline • pranny • prat • prawn of pleasure • premises • pretty-pretty • prick holder • prick
purse • prick scourer • prick skinner • prides • prime
cut • private parts • private passages • private property •
privates • privities • privy chose • privy hole • privy
members • privy parts • promised land • pubes • pu-
bickers • pubis • pudendal inlet • pudendal sanctum •
pudendal smile • pudendum • puff • puka • pulpit • pum-
pum • pump • pun pun • punani • punce • punni • punse •
purse • puss • pussy • pussy beard • pussy cover • pussy
hair • pussycat • puta

Q

quaint • quarry • queen of holes • queynte • quid • quiff •
quim • quim bush • quim whiskers • quim wig • quiver

R

rabbit pie • rag box • rails • rasp • rat hole • rattlesnake canyon • receiving chamber • receiving set • receptive pudendum • red ace • red lane • red snapper • reproductive organs • rhubarb • road • road to heaven • road to paradise • road to a christening • rob the ruffian • rocket socket • rose • rosebud • rosebush • rotten crotch • rough-and-ready • rough-and-tumble • rough-o • rubyfruit • rubyfruit jungle • rude bits • rude parts • rug

S

sacred areas • saddle • saint's delight • salt basin • salt cellar • satin doll • sanctum • sardine can • satchel • scallops • scat • scratch • scut • scuttle • second belly button • second hole from the back of the neck • secret door • secret parts • secret works • secrets • see you next Tuesday • seed plot • seething gash • seminary • sensible part • sensitive spot • serpent socket • sex skin • sexual slit • shake bag • shame tongue • sharp and blunt • she-thing • sheer hell • Shooter's Hill • short and curlies • short hairs • shotlocker • shrubbery • sideways smile • silent beard • silent mouth • sink of solitude • skin chimney • skin coat • skins • skunt • slash • sleeve • slice of life • slime hole • slippery slued • slit • slit bit • slithery • slitted underbelly • sloppy bot • slot • sluice • sluice box • smell hole • smelly pussy • smoo • snackbar • snake pit • snapper • snapping pussy • snapping turtle • snatch • snatch blatch • snatch box • snatch patch • Snatchsquatch • snatch thatch • snippet • snizz • snutchie • soft furry mound of love • south pole • southern hemisphere • spadger • spare tongue • sperm bank • sperm canal • sperm sucker • spice of life • spittoon • split • split apricot • split beaver • split kipper • split tail • sporran • sportsman's gap • sportsman's hole • spot • spread • spunk pot • squeeky • squelchy monkey • squidge • squirrel • stadge • staff breaker • standing room for one • stank • star over the garter • steel woolies • stench trench • stink • stink hole • stink pit • stink pot • stink well • stoat • strawberry patch • streamstown • stubble • suck-and-swallow • sugar basin • sugar bowl • sugar bush • sugared diamond • sunny south • sweet potato • sweet-scented hole.

T

taco • tail • tail box • tail feathers • tail for the cock • tail hole • tail gap • tailgate • tailpipe • tail stew • target • tastebud • teazie • tee-tee • temple of low men • Temple of Virginity • tender box • tender button • tender trap • that there • that thing • thatch • thatch hatch • thatched house • thicket • thigh pie • thing • thingby • thing stable • thingamabob • third base • tickle-Thomas • tickler • till • tinderbox • tidbits • tirly-whirly • tit-bit • titmouse • tivvy • todger toaster • toolbox • tool chest • toolshed • toot toot • toothless mouth • tootsie-wootsie • touch hole • toupee • toy shop • tram line • trap • treasure • treasure box • treasury • trench • triangle of love • trigger • trim • trinket • Tropic of Pubes • trout • tube • tufted honor • tufted treasure • tulips • tuna • tuna fish • tuna taco • tuna town • tunnel • tunnel of love • tuppy • turnpike • turf • turtle • tuzzy-muzzy • twam • twammy • twat • twat fuzz • twat hair • twat mat • twat rug • twatchel • twidget • twim • twin • twitchet • twixt wind and water • two-leaved book • twot

U

undercarriage • undercut • undergrowth • underparts • undertaker • underworld • unit • unmentionables • upright grin • upright wink • usher of the hall

V

vacuum • vadge • vag • vagina • vagina dentata • vaginal rim • vaginal hair • valentine • veedge • valley • valley of love • valve • VD depository • Velcro love triangle • Velcro strips • velvet glove • velvet love canal • velvet tunnel • venerable monosyllable • vent • Venus flytrap • Venus mound • Venus' cell • Venus' glove • Venus highway • Venus' honeypot • Venus' mark • Venus' secret cell • vertical axe wound with sideburns • vertical bacon baguette • vertical bacon sandwich • vertical smile • vicious circle • virgin treasure • Virginia vagina • vitals • volcano • vulvar interlabial slit • vulvette

W

wares • warm fuzzy • warm place • warm spot • warmest place • waste pipe • water box • water engine • water worker • waterworks • way in • wayside fountain • wet mop • wet-on • wetlands • whatchamacallit • whatsis • whatsit • whatzis • wheel • whelk • where the monkey sleeps • where uncle's doodle goes • whidgey • whim • whim-wham • whisker biscuit • whisker pot • whisker temple of delight • whisper pot • whole • whole voyage • wicket • wide-on • wig • wings of the vulva • winker • wishing well • woman's commodity • woman's privates • woman's privities • wonderland • woo-woo • wool •

woolies • wools • workshop • world's smallest hotel • wound • wrinkle • wuzzy

X

X marks the spot

Y

Y-bone • Y-bone steakhouse • yard measure • yawn • yeast bag • yeast mill • yellow road • YMCA • yogurt factory • yoni • you-know-what • you-know-where • yum-yum • yum-yum cake

Z

zatch • zebra fanny • zither • zouzoune

• •

THINGS AND THE GUYS THEY WERE NAMED FOR

America	Amerigo Vespucci, explorer
Chrysler	Walter Chrysler, engineer and auto manufacturer
Colt Firearms	Samuel Colt, gun maker
Dodge	Dodge brothers, John and Horace, automakers
Diesel	Rudolf Diesel, inventor
Disneyland	Walt Disney, cartoonist
Doberman	Ludwig Doberman, German dog breeder

Dow Jones	Charles Dow and Edward Jones, financial journalists
Eiffel Tower	Gustave Eiffel, architect
Edsel	Edsel Ford, automaker
Ferrari	Enzo Ferrari, automaker
Ferris wheel	George Ferris, Jr., inventor
Ford Motor Co.	Henry Ford, automaker
Fender guitars	Leo Fender, guitar maker
Forbes magazine	B. C. Forbes, publisher
Gibson guitars	Orville Gibson, guitar maker
Gore-Tex	Wilbert Gore, inventor
Harley-Davidson	William Harley, Arthur Davidson, motorcycle makers
Hershey bar	Milton S. Hershey, candy maker
Hilton hotels	Barron Hilton, hotel operator
JC Penney	John Cash Penney, merchant
Les Paul guitars	Lester Polfus (Les Paul), guitarist and designer
Marriott Hotels	James Marriott, hotel operator
Marshall amplifiers	Jim Marshall, amp maker
Mount Everest	Sir George Everest, surveyor
Oldsmobile	Rasom E. Olds (also known as REO), automaker
Saxophone	Adolphe Sax, inventor
Salmonella	Daniel Salmon, researcher
Stradivarius violin	Antonio Stradivari, instrument maker
Tesla Coil	Nikola Tesla, inventor
Uzi	Uziel Gal, gun designer
Wal-Mart	Sam Walton, founder
Warner Bros.	Jack, Sam, Harry, and Albert Warner, film moguls

DRESSING UP AND GOING OUT

Black tie: formal. A tuxedo is required, and might include more formal tuxedos, such as evening tails. Women wear cocktail dresses, long dresses, or dressy evening separates.

White tie: ultra-formal. Men wear full tails with white tie, vest, shirt. Women wear long gowns.

Formal: the same as black tie, but in trendier cities like New York or Los Angeles, it could mean a black shirt with a tux, possibly without a tie. Women wear cocktail or long dresses.

Black tie optional or black tie invited: tuxedo optional, although a dark suit and tie is acceptable. Women wear cocktail or long dresses.

Creative black tie: trendy formal, à la New York or L.A., such as a tux with black shirt and no tie. Women wear cocktail or long dresses or something incredibly trendy.

Semi-formal: the trickiest of all dress codes. Usually tuxes are not required, but evening events still mean a dark suit. Daytime semi-formal events mean a suit, although not necessarily a dark suit. For women, both events means elegant short dress or dressy suit.

Cocktail attire: a dark suit. Women wear elegant shorter dresses.

Dressy casual: no jeans or shorts. Not quite as casual as business casual.

Casual: anything goes.

Informal: casual. However, when associated with a

wedding or other special event, dress slacks and button-front shirt are the norm.

When in doubt, ask the hosts of the party or other guests before the event. It's usually better to be overdressed than underdressed.

• •

MANAGEMENT VS. EMPLOYEES

Unless you won the genetic lotto, odds are that your first job out of college is not going to land you an office on executive row. So, you need to get used to swallowing a little crow—and smiling as it goes down. It's going to be tough, especially if you work for a nitwit, but there are ways around it. Verbal sleight-of-hand is an excellent way to maintain your dignity while appearing to bow to the company's wishes. Here's our preferred way: use the phrase in the first column while keeping the second phrase—the one you want to say—in the back of your mind.

For those of you already in management, use this list as a cheat sheet, sort of like a secret decoder ring that will help you figure out just what the fuck your underlings are thinking.

WHAT TO SAY	WHAT IT MEANS
I'm not certain that's feasible.	No fucking way.
I don't think you understand.	Shove it up your ass.
Really?	You've got to be shitting me.
Perhaps you should check with . . .	Tell someone who gives a fuck.
Of course I'm concerned.	Ask me if I give a fuck.
I wasn't involved in that project.	It's not my fucking problem.
Interesting behavior.	What the fuck?
I'm not sure I can implement this.	Fuck it, it won't work.
I'll try to schedule that.	Why the fuck didn't you tell me that sooner?
Perhaps I can work late.	When the fuck do you expect me to do this?
Are you sure it's a problem?	Who the fuck cares?
He's not familiar with that problem.	He's got his head up his ass.
You don't say.	Eat shit.
Excuse me?	Eat shit and die.
Excuse me, sir?	Eat shit and die, motherfucker.
They weren't happy with it?	What the fuck do they want from me?
So you'd like help with it?	Kiss my ass.
I'm on salary and I'm a bit overloaded at the moment.	Fuck it.

WHAT TO SAY	WHAT IT MEANS
You want me to take care of this?	Who the hell died and made you boss?
Yes, we should discuss this.	Great, another fucking meeting.
I don't think it will be a problem.	I really don't give a shit.
How nice. How very nice.	Fuck you.
I see.	Blow me.
Do you see?	Blow yourself.
I love a challenge.	This job sucks.

• •

WORDS OF WISDOM: RESUMES

Your resume should be only one page in length. If it's two pages, it's going to go into the circular file. No one has time to read two pages—of anything. So make it short, but make it good. State specifically what you want to do, what jobs you've had in the past along with the responsibilities each entailed, and then offer your references "upon request." Skip the "married with children, loves to golf" crap. You can talk about that at the interview.

And never, ever lie on your resume. You can leave things out, but don't make stuff up. If you do, it will come back to haunt you.

MASTURBATION SLANG

auditioning your finger puppets • balling off • bang the banjo • bash the bishop • beat it • beat the meat • beating off • bitchslapping your uncle • bleed the serpent • bop the baloney • buffing the pickle • burp the worm • butter the lobster • Captain Jack personified • change gears • chase the weasel • choke the bishop • choking the bald guy until he pukes • choking the chicken • choking the chipmunk • choking the gopher • chuck one's muck • cracking nuts • dancing with Rosie and her five daughters • date with Rosy Palms • dick off • doing battle with the purple-helmeted warrior of love • dolloping the wiener • dunk your dolphin • fist rape • fisting off • five against one • five knuckle chuckle • five knuckle shuffle • five knuckle shuffle on the old piss pipe • flog the dolphin • flog the dong • flog the log • flogging the meat • flogging the poodle • graze a knuckle • grease the axle • grease the sprocket • hand-shandy • having one off the wrist • having a tug • hitting a home run at the T-ball game • jack off • jacking the beanstalk • jerking off • jerkin' the gherkin • make the bald man cry • making the camel spit • onanism • one-handed pink pole vaulting • peel the banana • performing diagnostics on your man tool • petting the one-eyed trouser snake • play the upright organ • playing tag with the pink torpedo • pocket billiards • pocket pool (through the clothing) • polish the knob • polish the low-quarters • polish the purple helmet • polish the wahd • polishing the silver • plug the melon • pull one's pud • pull the peter •

punch the clown • rub one out • self-service • shaking hands with Abraham Lincoln • sling jelly • spanking the frank • spanking the monkey • spunk up • squeeze one off • squeeze the lotion dispenser • squeezing the tomato • squeezing the tube • squirt around • stroke • stroke it • stroke off • stroke the salami • strum the strudel • teaching cyclops the lambada • tickling the turkey • toss off • twisting the knob • walk the dog • wank • wank off • wax the dolphin • wax the rod • whack off • whacking the weasel • whip the birdie • whistle Dixie • working out your problems • yank off • yanking the chain

ANNIVERSARY GIFTS

You may not care, but your significant other sure will.

	TRADITIONAL	MODERN	ALT. MODERN
1	**paper**	**plastics**	**clocks**
2	cotton	cotton/calico	china
3	leather	leather	crystal/glass
4	flowers	linen/silk/nylon	appliances
5	**wood**	**wood**	**silverware**
6	candy/iron	iron	wood
7	copper/wool	copper/wool/brass	desk sets
8	bronze/pottery	bronze/appliances	linens
9	pottery/willow	pottery	leather
10	**tin**	**aluminum**	**diamond**

	TRADITIONAL	MODERN	ALT. MODERN
11	steel	steel	jewelry
12	silk/linen	silk/linen	pearl
13	lace	lace	textiles/fur
14	ivory	ivory	gold
15	**crystal**	**glass**	**watches**
20	**china**	**china**	**platinum**
25	**silver**	**silver**	**silver**
30	pearl	pearl	pearl
35	coral	coral/jade	jade
40	ruby	ruby/garnet	ruby
45	sapphire	sapphire	sapphire
50	**gold**	**gold**	**gold**
55	emerald	emerald/turquoise	emerald
60	**diamond**	**gold**	**diamond**
75	diamond	diamond/gold	diamond

By the way, only eight are official (noted in bold). The rest were concocted by female "feel good" companies like Hallmark. Surprised?

COCKTAILS

BLOODY MARY

1¼ oz. vodka, dash of lemon juice, dash of Worcestershire sauce or 3 drops Tabasco, pepper, salt or celery salt, 8 oz. tomato juice

Pour vodka followed by tomato juice over ice in a tall glass. Add spices to taste. Stir vigorously, garnish with lime wedge. Celery stick if someone really wants the vegetables. NOTE: Using clamato juice creates a Bloody Caesar.

COSMOPOLITAN

4 parts vodka, 2 parts Cointreau or triple sec, 1 part lime juice, 2 parts cranberry juice

Shake and strain into a chilled cocktail glass. Serve with a lime wedge.

GIBSON

2 oz. gin or vodka, dash of dry vermouth

Stir with ice and strain into a chilled cocktail glass. Garnish with skewered cocktail onions.

NOTE: No vermouth if ordered dry.

GIMLET

1½ oz. gin or vodka, splash of lime juice

Stir with ice and serve on the rocks in a lowball glass, or strain into a chilled cocktail glass. Garnish with a lime wedge.

HIGHBALL

1¼ oz. any liquor; water, ginger ale, 7-Up, or soda

Build with liquor of your choice in a highball glass filled with ice.

KAMIKAZE

1 oz. vodka, ¾ oz. triple sec, dash of lime juice and sour mix

Shake with ice, strain into a chilled cocktail glass.

LONG ISLAND ICED TEA

¾ oz. each: rum, gin, vodka, tequila, and triple sec, sour mix, and a splash of cola

Shake liquors together with sour mix. Pour in large glass. Add splash of cola, garnish with lemon wedge.

MANHATTAN

1½ oz. whiskey or bourbon, ¾ oz. sweet vermouth, a dash of bitters (optional)

Build in a rocks glass or stir over ice. Strain into a chilled cocktail glass to serve. Garnish with a cherry.

NOTE: A "Perfect Manhattan" uses equal parts of sweet and dry vermouth, and is garnished with a lemon twist.

MARTINI

2 oz. gin, ½ oz. vermouth

Stir over ice and strain into a chilled cocktail glass. Garnish with a spear of olives. For a dry martini, leave out the vermouth and garnish with a lemon twist. Use vodka instead of gin for a vodka martini.

SALTY DOG

1 1/4 oz. gin, grapefruit juice
Pour in highball glass rimmed with salt, over ice.

TOM COLLINS

1 1/4 oz. gin, sour mix, splash of soda
Shake gin and sour mix with ice. Pour into a collins glass (tall, thin glass). Top with soda, garnish with an orange slice and a cherry.

• •

NASCAR CHAMPIONS

YEAR	DRIVER	MAKE	CHAMPIONSHIP
2007	Jimmy Johnson	Chevrolet	Nextel cup
2006	Jimmy Johnson	Chevrolet	Nextel Cup
2005	Tony Stewart	Chevrolet	Nextel Cup
2004	Kurt Busch	Ford	Nextel Cup
2003	Matt Kenseth	Ford	Winston Cup
2002	Tony Stewart	Pontiac	Winston Cup
2001	Jeff Gordon	Chevrolet	Winston Cup
2000	Bobby Labonte	Pontiac	Winston Cup
1999	Dale Jarrett	Ford	Winston Cup
1998	Jeff Gordon	Chevrolet	Winston Cup
1997	Jeff Gordon	Chevrolet	Winston Cup
1996	Terry Labonte	Chevrolet	Winston Cup
1995	Jeff Gordon	Chevrolet	Winston Cup
1994	Dale Earnhardt	Chevrolet	Winston Cup
1993	Dale Earnhardt	Chevrolet	Winston Cup

YEAR	DRIVER	MAKE	CHAMPIONSHIP
1992	Alan Kulwicki	Ford	Winston Cup
1991	Dale Earnhardt	Chevrolet	Winston Cup
1990	Dale Earnhardt	Chevrolet	Winston Cup
1989	Rusty Wallace	Pontiac	Winston Cup
1988	Bill Elliott	Ford	Winston Cup
1987	Dale Earnhardt	Chevrolet	Winston Cup
1986	Dale Earnhardt	Chevrolet	Winston Cup
1985	Darrell Waltrip	Chevrolet	Winston Cup
1984	Terry Labonte	Chevrolet	Winston Cup
1983	Bobby Allison	Buick	Winston Cup
1982	Darrell Waltrip	Buick	Winston Cup
1981	Darrell Waltrip	Buick	Winston Cup
1980	Dale Earnhardt	Chevrolet	Winston Cup
1979	Richard Petty	Chevrolet	Winston Cup
1978	Cale Yarborough	Oldsmobile	Winston Cup
1977	Cale Yarborough	Chevrolet	Winston Cup
1976	Cale Yarborough	Chevrolet	Winston Cup
1975	Richard Petty	Plymouth	Winston Cup
1974	Richard Petty	Plymouth	Winston Cup
1973	Benny Parsons	Chevrolet	Winston Cup
1972	Richard Petty	Plymouth	Winston Cup
1971	Richard Petty	Plymouth	Grand National
1970	Bobby Isaac	Dodge	Grand National
1969	David Pearson	Ford	Grand National
1968	David Pearson	Ford	Grand National
1967	Richard Petty	Plymouth	Grand National
1966	David Pearson	Dodge	Grand National
1965	Ned Jarrett	Ford	Grand National
1964	Richard Petty	Plymouth	Grand National
1963	Joe Weatherly	Pontiac	Grand National
1962	Joe Weatherly	Pontiac	Grand National

YEAR	DRIVER	MAKE	CHAMPIONSHIP
1961	Ned Jarrett	Chevrolet	Grand National
1960	Rex White	Chevrolet	Grand National
1959	Lee Petty	Plymouth	Grand National
1958	Lee Petty	Oldsmobile	Grand National
1957	Buck Baker	Chevrolet	Grand National
1956	Buck Baker	Chrysler	Grand National
1955	Tim Flock	Chrysler	Grand National
1954	Lee Petty	Chrysler	Grand National
1953	Herb Thomas	Hudson	Grand National
1952	Tim Flock	Hudson	Grand National
1951	Herb Thomas	Hudson	Grand National
1950	Bill Rexford	Oldsmobile	Grand National
1949	Red Byron	Oldsmobile	Strictly Stock

In 2004, Nextel took over the title cup sponsorship from Winston. In 2008, the name was changed to the Sprint Cup after Nextel's merger with Sprint.

• • • • • • • • •

FUCK

From a man's perspective, the most versatile word in the English language is the word "fuck." It is the one word that can convey pain and pleasure, love and hate.

Grammatically, "fuck" falls into many categories. It can be a noun (Jane is a terrific fuck) and a verb (Dick regularly fucks up). It can be both a transitive verb (Dick fucked Jane) and intransitive verb (Jane was fucked by Dick). It can also be an action verb (Dick really gives a fuck) and a passive verb (Jane really doesn't give a fuck). It works as an adverb (Jane is pretty fucking interested in Dick) and as an adjective (Jane gives the best fucking blowjobs on the planet). It can be used alone as an interjection (Fuck! I'm late for my date with Jane). It can also be used as a form of subordinating conjunction (Jane is easy but, fuck, she's also stupid) or the basis for a question (What the fuck?). It can even be inserted into words to create new ones (Unbefuckinglievable! Fanfuckingtastic! Absofuckinglutely. Infuckingcredible!).

It can even be used as almost every word in a sentence, (although this is not advised). "Fuck you, you fucking fuck" and "That fucking fuck-up fucked this fucker up again."

Fuck can also be used in place of many standard and less extreme words to more specifically provide description and convey a wide range of emotions. For example:

Aggression: Fuck you.

Agreement: Fucking-ay.

Amazement: Fucking shit!

Annoyance: Don't fuck with me.

Apathy: Who really gives a fuck, anyway?

Benevolence: Don't do me any fucking favors.

Command: Go fuck yourself.

Confusion: What the fuck?

Denial: I didn't fucking do it.

Despair: Fucked again.

Difficulty: I don't understand this fucking thing.

Directions: Fuck off.

Disbelief: No fucking way!

Dismay: I can't fucking believe this.

Displeasure: What the fuck is going on here?

Encouragement: Keep on fucking.

Etiquette: Pass the fucking salt.

Fraud: I got fucked.

Greetings: How the fuck are you?

Hatred of chemistry: Thermofuckingdynamics.

Identification: Who the fuck is this?

Ignorance: He's such a fuck head.

Incompetence: He's a fuck-up.

Insight: You're out of your fucking mind.

Laziness: He's a fuck-off.

Lost: Where the fuck are we?

Panic: Let's get the fuck out of here.

Passive: Fuck me.

Philosophical: Who gives a fuck?

Pleasure: I couldn't be any fucking happier.

Question: You aren't fucking with me, are you?

Rebellion: Fuck the world!

Resignation: Fuck this.

Retaliation: Up your fucking ass.

Suspicion: Who the fuck are you?

Trouble: I guess I'm fucked now.

Ugliness—You're a dumb-looking fuck.

Wisdom—Fuck that shit.

Wonder—How the fuck did you do that?

ASIMOV'S THREE LAWS OF ROBOTICS

A robot may not injure a human being, or, through inaction, allow a human being to come to harm.

A robot must obey the orders given it by human beings except where such orders would conflict with the First Law.

A robot must protect its own existence as long as such protection does not conflict with the First or Second Law.

COMPUTER TERMS

When you're talking about the size of your hard drive or how incredibly huge your memory is, you use the following terms. They usually come before the word "byte" (a byte is about how much memory it takes to represent a single letter, like "A"). Enterprising men can also use these prefixes to represent amounts of money in their bank accounts ("megamillions"), or the level of hotness found in supermodels and porn stars ("terababe").

kilo (K)	1 thousand (3 zeroes)
mega (M)	1 million (6 zeroes)
giga (G)	1 billion (9 zeroes)

tera (T)	1 trillion (12 zeroes)
peta (P)	1 quadrillion (15 zeroes)
exa	1 quintillion (18 zeroes)
zetta	1 sextillion (21 zeroes)
yotta	1 septillion (24 zeroes)

A yottabyte equals 1,208,925,819,614,629,174,706,176 bytes.

• •

TERMS FOR SEXUAL INTERCOURSE

A

a bit of the old in and out • act of darkness • action • Adam and Eve it • all's well when ends meet

B

backseat mambo • bait the hook • baking cookies • ball • baloney ride • bananas and cream • bang • bash the beaver • be in a woman's beef • be up to one's balls • beast with two backs • beasty rendezvous • beat cheeks • beat her up with an ugly stick • bed boogie • bed-pressing • beef in your taco • belly ride • blanket drill • board • boff • boff your brains out • bohemian cluster fuck • boink • boom-boom • bone dance • bone her • bonk • boof • bop • bop her • bounce the mattress • breed • bump and grind • bump bellies • bump uglies • bumpin' fuzzies • bunny fuck • bury the baby leg • bury the beef • bury the bone • bury the weenie • bush patrol • butter the muffin • buzz the brillo

C

cane her • carnal gymnastics • carnal knowledge • clean her pipes • clean the carpet • coitus • copulate • couple with • crack it • cram • crashing the custard truck • cream her • creamin' • cut the mustard

D

dance the buttock jig • dance the matrimonial polka • dance the mattress jig • dancing in the sheets • diddle • dip your stick • dip your stinger in the honey • dip your wick • dirty work at the crossroads • disappearing cane trick • dive in the dark • diving for pearls • do a lewd infusion • do her • do it • do some ladies' tailoring • do the chores • do the deed • do the hippity dippity • do the old in-out • do the wild thing • doing the ugly • doing the nasty • doona dance • drill • drilling for oil • drilling the ditch • drive home • dust the broom

E

eat cauliflower • eat hymeneal sweets • effing • engage the enemy • enjoin • enjoy a flesh session • exchange bodily fluids

F

featherbed jig • feed the dummy • feed the kitty • fill the void • filling the cream doughnut • fit end to end • fit her clap flap • fix her plumbing • flesh Session • flop • flop in the hay • fornication • four-legged frolic • frigging • front door action • fuck • the funky chicken

G

genital exercise • get a belly full of marrow pudding • get a shove in your blind eye • get creamy • get down • get into her pants • get it on • get Jack in the orchard • get laid • get lucky • get some stank on the hang low • get oats from her • get some ass • get stretched • get your chimney swept out • get your end wet • get your hair cut • get your jollies • get your leather stretched • get your nuts cracked • get your oil changed • get your pole varnished • get your rocks off • getting some • give a hole to hide in • give a woman a shot • give hard for soft • give her a hosing • give her a pat • give her a stab • give her the business • give her the high hard one • give juice for jelly • give pussy a taste of cream • give her the works • give the dog a bone • glazing the donut • go all the way • go belly-to-belly • go fishing • go like a belt-fed motor • go like a rat up a drainpipe • go to bed with • go to town • goose her • grease her • grease the wheel • grind • grind your tool • growling at the badger

H

hammer • hammer her • hanky panky • haul your ashes • have a bit of curly greens • have a bit of fish • have a bit of giblet pie • have a bit of pork • have a bit of split mutton • have a bit of sugar stick • have a bit of summer cabbage • have a bit of the cramstick • have a hot roll with cream • have a joyride • have a piece of tail • have a poke • have a squeeze and a squirt • have a turn on your

back • have sex with • hide the ferret • horizontal re-
freshment • hide the salami • hide the sausage • hippity
dippity • hit it • hokey-pokey • home run • hop on the
good foot and do the bad thing • horizontal bop • horizontal exercises • horizontal hokey pokey • horizontal
hula • horizontal mambo • horizontal polka • horizontal
tango • horizontalize • hose her • hot dog in a jungle •
hump • humpity dumpity • the humpty dance • Humpty
Dumpty

I

impale her • intercourse • introduce Charlie

J

jab her • jazz • jiggle her • jink • join paunches • joyride •
juice her • jump her bones

K

knock boots • knocking mops • know her—in the Bibli-
cal sense

L

land the plane • lay • lay some pipe • leap • lie feet up •
lie with • lift a leg on her • light the lamp • lose the match
and pocket the stake

M

make baskets • make ends meet • make grass sand-
wiches • make her grunt • make it • make the sign of the
humpbacked whale • makin' bacon • making babies •

making it • making love • making whoopee • mate • mat-rimonial polka • mattress dancing • mattress mambo • mingle limbs • mix your peanut butter • mommy-daddy dance • mount • mucking around

N

nail • nail two bellies together • the nasty • the naughty • nibble her • nookie • nooner (daytime only) • nose painting

O

offshore drilling

P

parallel park • park the hot rod • parking the car • park-ing the beef bus in tuna town • parking the pink Ply-mouth in the garage of love • parking the yacht in Hair Harbor • parting the Pink Sea • pass the gravy • peel your best end • peg • penetration • phallicize her • picnic in the lawn • pile driving • pin • plant a man • plant the oats • plant your seed • play at in-and-out • play at tops-and-bottoms • play cars and garages • play doctor • play hide the bone • play hide the hot dog • play hide the wee-nie • play on the hair court • play pickle-me, tickle-me • play tiddlywinks • plook • plow her • plug and play • plug her • poke her • poke in the whiskers • polish the rocket • pop her • pop it in • pork • pound her • pray with the knees upward • press bellies • probing the membrane • professional wrestling • pump her • put the bee in the hive • put the boots to her • put the devil into Hell • put your root down • put your snake in the grass • puttin' on the ritz • putting sour cream in the burrito • putting the candle in the pumpkin • putting the tool in the shed

Q

quickie • quimsticking

R

rail • ram • ramming the rod • randadan 'til the cows come home • ream • ride • ride the hobby horse • ride the baloney pony • ride the pink pony • ride the skin bus to Tuna Town • ring her bell • roast the broomstick • rock and roll • rock the casabah • roll in the hay • romp • roughin' up the suspect • rub bacons • rub one out • rumble • rump splitting • rump work • rutting

S

saucing the clam • saw off a chunk • schtupp her • score • screw • scrog • sew a hole • sexercize • shaft • shag • shake a skin coat • shake the sheets • shoot the moon • shoot your wad • shucking the oyster • sink it in • sink the pink • sink the sausage • sink the soldier • slam • slap the slot • slap skins • slap some skin • slash the gash • sleeping with • slip her a length • slip her the hot beef injection • slip into • smashing pissers • sow your (wild) oats • spanking the cat • spear the bearded clam • split • squat jumps in the cucumber patch • squatting on the hog • squeeze and a squirt • stabbing the trout • stargazing on your back • stir the macaroni • storm the trenches • stretch leather • stuffing • stuff the beaver •

stuff the taco • suck the sugar-stick • swiping the V-card • swing

T

take a belly-ride • take a turn in the stubble • take a turn on Shooter's Hill • take it to the car wash • take the jism trail • take the starch out of her • taking a break • taking "old one-eye" to the optometrist • taking the flesh boat to Tuna Town • tear off a piece • tear the sheets • tell a bed-time story • thread • thread the needle • throw a leg over • throw another log on the fire • throw the dagger • throw the meat at her • thump • tie the true lover's knot • tooling in the bush • tops and bottoms • trade a bit of hard for a bit of soft • train through a tunnel • trim • trim the buff • twat raking • twiddle • two-backed beast • two in the pink, one in the stink

U

up to ya nuts in guts • uppy downy

V

varnish your cane • visit the Netherlands • vitamin F

W

walk the dog • wallpaper the closet • water the lawn • wet your wick • what mother did before me • whitewash her • the wild thing • wind up the clock • windsurfing on Mount Baldy • wink wink, nudge nudge • work the hairy oracle • workout

X

X-axis grind

Y

yodel in the valley • yodeling in the gulley

Z

zallywhacking • Ziggy-wiggling • zoinkering • zwoosh-ing the swoosh

• •

WORDS OF WISDOM: SEX

Show me a beautiful woman with a boyfriend, and I'll show you a guy who's already tired of fucking her.

• •

TOP GUY MOVIES

If you haven't seen every one of these, take a month off, load up the refrigerator with beer, and get out the remote.

Alien
Animal House
Apocalypse Now
Black Hawk Down

Blazing Saddles
Cool Hand Luke
The Deer Hunter
Die Hard
Dirty Harry
Fight Club
The French Connection
Gladiator
The Godfather
Goldfinger
The Great Escape
Lethal Weapon
The Longest Yard
The Matrix
The Maltese Falcon
The Mechanic
Monty Python and the Holy Grail
National Lampoon's *Vacation*
Rambo
Reservoir Dogs
The Road Warrior
Robocop
Rocky
Scarface
Stripes
The Terminator
This Is Spinal Tap
Top Gun
The Wild Bunch

GREAT PROFESSIONAL WRESTLERS AND THEIR SIGNATURE MOVES

Bruno Sammartino (1960s–80s): Sammartino Slam (front powerslam)

George "The Animal" Steele (1960s–80s): Flying hammerlock

Dusty Rhodes (1960s–90s): American Elbow (modified elbow drop)

Andre the Giant (1970s–80s): Andre Driver (modified belly-to-belly piledriver)

Larry Zbyszko (1970s–80s): The Larry Land Dreamer (modified guillotine choke)

"Rowdy" Roddy Piper (1970s–80s): piledriver, sleeper hold

Randy "Macho Man" Savage (1970s–90s): Savage Strikes

"The Enforcer" Arn Anderson (1980s–90s): Spinebuster

Bret "Hitman" Hart (1980s–90s): Sharpshooter (scorpion hold)

The Ultimate Warrior (1980s–90s): gorilla press drop, running big splash

Hulk Hogan (1980s–90s): The Atomic Leg Drop

Bill Goldberg (1980s–90s): Jackhammer (suplex powerslam)

Chris Benoit (1980s–2000s): Crippler Crossface (modified arm trap crossface)

"The Nature Boy" Ric Flair (1980s–2000s): Figure Four Leglock

Stone Cold Steve Austin (1990s–2000s): Stone Cold Stunner (modified jawbreaker)

MALE NIPPLES

There is one question that has haunted men since they discovered the wonder of naked female breasts: why do guys have nipples, too? The medical community isn't sure: some researchers believe that it may be vestigial, like an appendix, with some purpose in our distant past. Others believe that they are simply a shared trait with females—like organs, limbs, etc.—but aren't "functioning" because men don't have enough estrogen to kick us into the league of breast-feeders. For modern men, nipples are little more than a source of amusement. However, they can cause excruciating pain during puberty if bumped (due to heightened sensitivity), they might bleed during marathons (nipple chafing), and they can even be aroused during sex. Really, that's all science knows and it's everything you need to know.

HEAVYWEIGHT BOXING CHAMPIONS

CHAMPION	ORGANIZATION*	YEARS
John L. Sullivan		1882–1892
James J. Corbett		1892–1897
Bob Fitzsimmons		1897–1899
James J. Jeffries		1899–1905, retired
Marvin Hart		1905–1906

CHAMPION	ORGANIZATION*	YEARS
Tommy Burns		1906–1908
Jack Johnson		1908–1915
Jess Willard		1915–1919
Jack Dempsey		1919–1926
Gene Tunney		1926–1928, retired
VACANT		1928–1930
Max Schmeling		1930–1932
Jack Sharkey		1932–1933
Primo Carnera		1933–1934
Max Baer		1934–1935
James J. Braddock		1935–1937
Joe Louis		1937–1949, retired
Ezzard Charles	NBA	1949–1950
Ezzard Charles		1950–1951
Jersey Joe Walcott		1951–1952
Rocky Marciano		1952–1956, retired undefeated
Floyd Patterson		1956–1959
Ingemar Johansson		1959–1960
Floyd Patterson		1960–1962
Sonny Liston		1962–1964
Muhammed Ali		1964–1965
Ernie Terrell	WBA	1965–1967
Muhammed Ali	WBC	1965–1967
Muhammed Ali		1967
VACANT		1967–1968
Joe Frazier	NYSAC	1968–1970
Jimmy Ellis	WBA	1968–1970

CHAMPION	ORGANIZATION*	YEARS
Joe Frazier		1970–1973
George Foreman		1973–1974
Muhammed Ali		1974–1978
Leon Spinks		1978
Leon Spinks	WBA	1978
Ken Norton	WBC	1978
Muhammed Ali	WBA	1978–1979, retired
Larry Holmes	WBC	1978–1983
John Tate	WBA	1979–1980
Mike Weaver	WBA	1980–1982
Michael Dokes	WBA	1982–1983
Gerrie Coetzee	WBA	1983–1984
Tim Witherspoon	WBC	1983–1984
Tim Witherspoon	WBA	1983–1984
Larry Holmes	IBF	1983–1985
Greg Page	WBA	1984–1985
Pinklon Thomas	WBC	1984–1986
Tony Tubbs	WBA	1985–1986
Michael Spinks	IBF	1985–1987
Trevor Berbick	WBC	1986
James "Bonecrusher" Smith	WBA	1986–1987
Mike Tyson	WBC	1986–1990
Tony Tucker	IBF	1987
Mike Tyson	WBA	1987–1990
Mike Tyson	IBF	1987–1990
Mike Tyson		1987–1990
James Buster Douglas		1990
Evander Holyfield		1990–1992

CHAMPION	ORGANIZATION*	YEARS
Riddick Bowe		1992
Riddick Bowe	WBA / IBF	1992–1993
Lennox Lewis	WBC	1992–1994
Evander Holyfield	WBA / IBF	1993–1994
Michael Moorer	WBA / IBF	1994
Oliver McCall	WBC	1994–1995
George Foreman	WBA / IBF	1994–1995
Francois Botha	IBF	1995–1996
Bruce Seldon	WBA	1995–1996
Frank Bruno	WBC	1995–1996
Mike Tyson	WBC	1996
Mike Tyson	WBA	1996
Michael Moorer	IBF	1996–1997
Evander Holyfield	WBA	1996–1999
VACANT	WBC	1996–1997
Lennox Lewis	WBC	1997–2001
Evander Holyfield	IBF	1997–1999
Evander Holyfield	WBA / IBF	1997–1999
Lennox Lewis		1999–2000
Lennox Lewis	WBC / IBF	1999–2001
VACANT	WBA	2000
Evander Holyfield	WBA	2000–2001
John Ruiz	WBA	2001–2003
Hasim Rahman	WBC / IBF	2001
Lennox Lewis	WBC / IBF	2001–2002
VACANT	IBF	2002
Lennox Lewis	WBC	2001–2004
Chris Byrd	IBF	2002–2006
Roy Jones, Jr.	WBA	2003–2004
John Ruiz	WBA	2004–2005
Vitali Klitschko	WBC	2004–2005

CHAMPION	ORGANIZATION*	YEARS
James Toney	WBA	2005
Hasim Rahman	WBC	2005–2006
Nikolay Valuev	WBA	2006
Wladimir Klitschko	IBF	2006
Oleg Maskaev	WBC	2006–2007
Rusian Chagaev	WBA	2007

* Where the organization is "blank," recognition was universal.

• •

IVY LEAGUE SCHOOLS

University of Pennsylvania (Philadelphia, PA)
Columbia University (Manhattan, NY)
Yale University (New Haven, CT)
Harvard University (Cambridge, MA)
Brown University (Providence, RI)
Princeton University (Princeton, NJ)
Cornell University (Ithaca, NY)
Dartmouth College (Hanover, NH)

• • • • • • • • • • •

PAC 10

Washington State University
University of Washington
Oregon State University

University of Oregon
University of California—Berkeley
Stanford University
University of California—Los Angeles
University of Southern California
Arizona State University
University of Arizona

• • • • • • • • • • •

BIG 10

University of Illinois
University of Indiana
University of Iowa
University of Michigan
Michigan State University
University of Minnesota
Northwestern University
Ohio State University
Penn State University
Purdue University
University of Wisconsin

The fact that there are eleven schools in the Big Ten is reflected in the Big Ten logo, which features the number "11" reversed out in the space between the "Big" and the "Ten."

MEET YOUR PROSTATE

Without question, the most uncomfortable and universal experience in every man's life is his prostate exam. You're supposed to get one when you turn forty years old, then every three to five years until you're fifty, then every two years after that. That's a lot of digital-rectal examinations between now and the time you cash in your chips, "digital-rectal examination" being the medical term for "having someone stick their finger up your ass."

So what's the deal with this digital-rectal examination? After all, most guys go through life committed to the fact that their assholes are "exit only." Having anyone—even a doctor—push his finger up your anus like it's a portal to the New World is a morbidly unpleasant thought that ranks up there with getting herpes. Like it or not, it's one of the best ways to detect prostate cancer, which is the most diagnosed cancer in the U.S. Prostate cancer is "man cancer," because the prostate is the gland that supplies fluid for sperm during ejaculation. In effect, it creates the juice in your jizz.

During the exam, the physician is merely touching your walnut-sized prostate trying to feel for hard spots or lumps. The doctor needs to prod the prostate—which is under your bladder and only accessible via the rectum—to make sure that it feels like it's in good shape. Doctors use lubrication and gloves to try and minimize the discomfort of this exam. Yet, there will be discomfort. You can count on that, although it's not as bad as, say, having your balls stepped on. You also should get a prostate-specific antigen blood test, called a PSA. This checks for high levels of prostate protein that can be an indication of cancer.

Many doctors believe that all men would get prostate cancer if they lived long enough. It might be nature's way of taking us out of the gene pool one at a time. The thinking goes like this: As men slow down reproductively (which is unavoidable since our bodies produce less testosterone as we age), our importance to the continued survival of the species diminishes. If we're not having ejaculations on a regular basis, then we're not creating offspring. So prostate cancer comes in to take us out of the gene pool like nature's very own hit man. Hey, you're not contributing—your time is up. You're gonna get whacked, literally. Bada bing, bada boom.

There is a theory that if you ejaculate regularly during your elderly years, you'll fool Mother Nature into believing that you're still an active member of the "I can reproduce" club. Even if you're eighty years old and don't have a living female partner, these theorists think that frequent ejaculation should still be achieved manually. Either way, shooting your wad could help delay the onset of prostate cancer. And if it doesn't, well, it's a good medical excuse for slamming the ham any time day or night.

Thousands of men's lives have been saved by routine prostate exams, and plenty more died because they didn't want to bend over and assume the position. There is, however, another option: prostate self-exams. The Internet has a number of sites that show you how you can do your own, as it were. Or you can convince your significant other to become proficient in slipping you the glove—the thought being that if you do it together, at least you'll get it done; sort of like guys giving breast exams.

One way or another, you're going to need to get that prostate examined. And someday, you'll look back on it and laugh. It just won't be the same day as the exam.

· ·

HAVING FUN WITH YOUR PROSTATE

The ten best things you can say to ease the tension during your prostate exam.

1) You know, doc, in Arkansas we're now legally married.
2) Any sign of the trapped miners, chief?
3) Oh boy, that was sphincterrific!
4) Are we there yet? Are we there yet? Are we there yet?
5) Take it easy, doc. You're boldly going where no man has gone before.
6) Whoo-hoo! Now I know how a Muppet feels!
7) Did you find Amelia Earhart yet?
8) If your hand doesn't fit, you must acquit!
9) Hey, doc, let me know if you find my dignity.
10) Could you write me a note for my wife saying that my head is not, in fact, up there?

PUBLIC ACTIVITIES TO AVOID IN THE PRESENCE OF YOUR WIFE

Lighting farts

Belching out loud

Spitting (for fun)

Spitting (for distance)

Pissing on the lawn

Whistling at other women

Joking about your wife's weight

Staring at other women's breasts

Commenting on other women's breasts

Taking note of how sexy your wife's sister is

Reminiscing about which old girlfriend was the best lay you ever had

Dancing only with single women at the neighborhood block party

Mentioning that the babysitter should show more cleavage

Asking the neighbors if they have sex more than you and the wife

Offering to "make it all better" for your wife's newly divorced best friend

HOTTEST FEMALE MUSICIANS

Deborah Harry (Blondie)
Beyoncé Knowles
Shania Twain
Chrissie Hynde (The Pretenders)
Janet Jackson
Kylie Minogue
Naomi Judd (the mom)

REASONS WHY IT'S GREAT TO BE A MAN

Your orgasms are real. Always.
Your last name stays with you after marriage.
The garage is all yours.
You never feel compelled to stop a friend from getting laid.
Car mechanics tell you the truth.
You don't give a shit if someone notices your new haircut.
Your ass is never a factor in a job interview.
Same work, more pay.
Wrinkles add character.
You don't have to leave the room to make emergency crotch adjustments.
If you retain water, it's in a bottle.

People never stare at your chest when you're talking to them.

One mood, all the time.

At a restaurant, you can go to the bathroom by yourself.

Phone conversations are over in sixty seconds or less.

A five-day vacation requires only one suitcase.

You can open all your own jars.

You get extra credit for minor, even thoughtless acts of thoughtfulness.

Your underwear is ten dollars for a three-pack.

If you are thirty-five and single, nobody notices. Or cares.

You can quietly enjoy a car ride from the passenger's seat.

No maxi-pads, tampons, or feminine hygiene sprays.

Three pairs of shoes are all you need.

You can quietly watch a game with a friend for hours without ever thinking, *He must be mad at me.*

If another guy shows up at the party in the same outfit, you just might become lifelong friends.

You are not expected to know the names of more than six colors.

You don't have to stop and think of which way to turn a nut on a bolt.

The same hairstyle lasts for years, maybe decades.

One color wallet, one pair of shoes—all year long.

You can "do" your nails with a pocketknife.

Hot wax never comes near your pubic area.

Wedding plans take care of themselves.

Wedding Dress $2000; Tux rental $100.

Christmas shopping can be accomplished for every relative in less than fifteen minutes on December twenty-fourth.

The world is your urinal.

HORSE RACING

Horse races are measured in furlongs. One furlong is equal to one-eighth of a mile (660 feet or 220 yards).

TYPES OF RACES:

Claiming: Any horse in the race may be purchased for a particular amount before the race. Claims made are announced after the race.

Handicap: Horses are assigned different weights to carry according to apparent ability (based on win record, etc.). This is done to even out the field.

Allowance: Horses are assigned weights according to factors stated in the race's entry conditions. Similar to handicap races, but uses a greater variety of qualifiers, such as age, sex, date of last race, etc.

Stakes: The big show. Financially and publicly the biggest races for horses, trainers, and owners. Money from entry fees is added to the purse.

TYPES OF BETS:

Win: Bettor picks a horse, and wins only if the horse finishes first.

Place: Bettor picks a horse, and wins if the horse finishes either first or second.

Show: Bettor picks a horse, and wins if the horse finishes first, second, or third.

Exacta: Bettor picks two horses and the order they will finish. Bettor wins if they finish first and second, in the right order.

Boxed exacta: Bettor picks two horses, and wins if they finish first and second in either order.

Trifecta: Bettor picks three horses and wins if they finish first, second, and third in the right order.

Daily Double: Bettor picks one horse in each of two races, and wins if they both finish first.

• •

THE TRIPLE CROWN

Triple Crown races are run with three-year-old thoroughbreds from early May to June.

Kentucky Derby: May at Churchill Downs in Louisville, Kentucky

Preakness Stakes: May at Pimlico Race Course in Baltimore, Maryland

Belmont Stakes: June at Belmont Park in Elmont, New York

Triple Crown winners:

1919   Sir Barton
1930   Gallant Fox
1935   Omaha
1937   War Admiral
1941   Whirlaway
1943   Count Fleet
1946   Assault
1948   Citation

1973   Secretariat
1977   Seattle Slew
1978   Affirmed

• • • • • • • • • • • • • • • •

WEATHER

Everyone talks about the weather, but no one does anything about it. Now, you'll be the only one who knows what he's talking about. Especially if you're the one that has to go out and shovel it.

RAIN

- **Sleet:** Raindrops that freeze into ice pellets before reaching the ground. Sleet usually bounces when hitting a surface and does not stick to objects.
- **Freezing rain:** Rain that falls onto a surface which has a temperature below freezing. This causes the rain to freeze to surfaces, such as trees, cars, and roads, forming a coating or glaze of ice.
- **Hail:** Raindrops that are blown up into the frigid area of a cloud. The raindrops freeze and then are coated with more water as they drop. They are then blown up again into the cloud, adding more layers of ice. When the hail gets too heavy to be blown upward, it falls to the ground. Hail ranges in size from a quarter of an inch to four inches in diameter.

SNOW

- **Blizzard:** Winds over 35 mph with snow (and blowing snow) reducing visibility to near zero.
- **Blowing snow:** Wind-driven snow that reduces visibility and causes significant drifting. Blowing snow may be snow that is falling and/or loose snow on the ground that is picked up by the wind.
- **Snow flurries:** Light snow falling for short periods of time. No accumulation, maybe light dusting on the ground.
- **Snow showers:** Snow falling at varying intensities for brief periods of time. Some accumulation is possible.

WINDS AND WAVES

- **Hurricane/Cyclone/Typhoon:** The terms "hurricane" and "typhoon" are regional names for a strong "tropical cyclone." All originate in tropical or subtropical waters and must spawn winds in excess of 74 mph. "Hurricane" is used in the North Atlantic Ocean; "typhoon" is used in the Pacific Ocean east of the international date line; "severe tropical cyclone" is used in the southwest Pacific Ocean and southeast Indian Ocean; "tropical cyclone" is used in the southwest Indian Ocean.
- **Tornado:** A violently rotating column of wind extending to the ground from the base of a thunderstorm cloud. Wind speeds can vary from 72 mph to almost 300 mph, however only about one percent of tornadoes in the U.S. reach 200 mph wind speeds. A tornado's intensity is measured on the Fujita wind damage scale. Most tornadoes occur in a region known as "Tornado Alley," from Nebraska to central Texas.

- **Tsunami:** A seismic sea wave that is generated by tectonic displacement of the seafloor from a volcano, landslide, or earthquake. This in turn causes a sudden displacement of the water above, and the resulting waves can be devastating to low-lying coastal areas.

• •

NBA BASKETBALL CHAMPIONSHIPS

YEAR	WINNER	RUNNER-UP	SERIES
2007	San Antonio	Cleveland	4-0
2006	Miami	Dallas	4-2
2005	San Antonio	Detroit	4-3
2004	Detroit	Los Angeles Lakers	4-1
2003	San Antonio	New Jersey	4-2
2002	Los Angeles Lakers	New Jersey	4-0
2001	Los Angeles Lakers	Philadelphia	4-1
2000	Los Angeles Lakers	Indiana	4-2
1999	San Antonio	New York	4-2
1998	Chicago	Utah	4-2
1997	Chicago	Utah	4-2
1996	Chicago	Seattle	4-2
1995	Houston	Orlando	4-0
1994	Houston	New York	4-3
1993	Chicago	Phoenix	4-2
1992	Chicago	Portland	4-2
1991	Chicago	Los Angeles Lakers	4-1
1990	Detroit	Portland	4-1
1989	Detroit	Los Angeles Lakers	4-0

YEAR	WINNER	RUNNER-UP	SERIES
1988	Los Angeles Lakers	Detroit	4-3
1987	Los Angeles Lakers	Boston	4-2
1986	Boston	Houston	4-2
1985	Los Angeles Lakers	Boston	4-2
1984	Boston	Los Angeles Lakers	4-3
1983	Philadelphia	Los Angeles Lakers	4-0
1982	Los Angeles Lakers	Philadelphia	4-2
1981	Boston	Houston	4-2
1980	Los Angeles Lakers	Philadelphia	4-2
1979	Seattle	Washington	4-1
1978	Washington	Seattle	4-3
1977	Portland	Philadelphia	4-2
1976	Boston	Phoenix	4-2
1975	Golden State	Washington	4-0
1974	Boston	Milwaukee	4-3
1973	New York	Los Angeles Lakers	4-1
1972	Los Angeles Lakers	New York	4-1
1971	Milwaukee	Baltimore	4-0
1970	New York	Los Angeles Lakers	4-3
1969	Boston	Los Angeles Lakers	4-3
1968	Boston	Los Angeles Lakers	4-2
1967	Philadelphia	San Francisco	4-2
1966	Boston	Los Angeles Lakers	4-3
1965	Boston	Los Angeles Lakers	4-1
1964	Boston	San Francisco	4-1
1963	Boston	Los Angeles Lakers	4-2
1962	Boston	Los Angeles Lakers	4-3
1961	Boston	St. Louis	4-1
1960	Boston	St. Louis	4-3
1959	Boston	Minneapolis	4-0
1958	St. Louis	Boston	4-2

YEAR	WINNER	RUNNER-UP	SERIES
1957	Boston	St. Louis	4-3
1956	Philadelphia	Fort Wayne	4-1
1955	Syracuse	Fort Wayne	4-3
1954	Minneapolis	Syracuse	4-3
1953	Minneapolis	New York	4-1
1952	Minneapolis	New York	4-3
1951	Rochester	New York	4-2
1950	Minneapolis	Syracuse	4-2
1949	Minneapolis	Washington	4-2
1948	Baltimore	Philadelphia	4-2
1947	Philadelphia	Chicago	4-1

NBA FINALS MOST VALUABLE PLAYERS

The NBA Finals Most Valuable Player Award is given to the player in the finals who contributed the most to the series.

YEAR	PLAYER	TEAM
2007	Tony Parker	San Antonio
2006	Dwyane Wade	Miami
2005	Tim Duncan	San Antonio
2004	Chauncey Billups	Detroit
2003	Tim Duncan	San Antonio
2002	Shaquille O'Neal	Los Angeles Lakers
2001	Shaquille O'Neal	Los Angeles Lakers
2000	Shaquille O'Neal	Los Angeles Lakers

YEAR	PLAYER	TEAM
1999	Tim Duncan	San Antonio
1998	Michael Jordan	Chicago
1997	Michael Jordan	Chicago
1996	Michael Jordan	Chicago
1995	Hakeem Olajuwon	Houston
1994	Hakeem Olajuwon	Houston
1993	Michael Jordan	Chicago
1992	Michael Jordan	Chicago
1991	Michael Jordan	Chicago
1990	Isiah Thomas	Detroit
1989	Joe Dumars	Detroit
1988	James Worthy	Los Angeles Lakers
1987	Magic Johnson	Los Angeles Lakers
1986	Larry Bird	Boston
1985	Kareem Abdul-Jabbar	Los Angeles Lakers
1984	Larry Bird	Boston
1983	Moses Malone	Philadelphia
1982	Magic Johnson	Los Angeles Lakers
1981	Cedric Maxwell	Boston
1980	Magic Johnson	Los Angeles Lakers
1979	Dennis Johnson	Seattle
1978	Wes Unseld	Washington
1977	Bill Walton	Portland
1976	Jo Jo White	Boston
1975	Rick Barry	Golden State
1974	John Havlicek	Boston
1973	Willis Reed	New York
1972	Wilt Chamberlain	Los Angeles Lakers
1971	Kareem Abdul-Jabbar	Milwaukee
1970	Willis Reed	New York
1969	Jerry West	Los Angeles Lakers

NBA CHAMPIONSHIPS BY FRANCHISE

TEAM	#	LAST	NOTABLE COACH
Boston Celtics	16	1986	K. C. Jones
Minneapolis—L.A. Lakers	14	2002	Pat Riley
Chicago Bulls	6	1998	Phil Jackson
Philadelphia—G.S. Warriors	3	1975	Al Attles
Syracuse Nats—Phil. 76ers	3	1983	Billy Cunningham
Detroit Pistons	3	2004	Chuck Daly
New York Knicks	2	1973	Red Holzman
Houston Rockets	2	1995	Rudy Tomjanovich
San Antonio Spurs	2	2005	Gregg Popovich
Baltimore Bullets*	1	1948	Buddy Jeannette
Milwaukee Bucks	1	1971	Larry Costello
Portland Trail Blazers	1	1977	Jack Ramsay
Rochester Royals—Sac. Kings	1	1951	Lester Harrison
St. Louis—Atlanta Hawks	1	1958	Alex Hannum
Seattle SuperSonics	1	1979	Lenny Wilkens
Washington Bullets	1	1978	Dick Motta

*Defunct

WASH YOUR HANDS

You don't wash your hands after taking a leak to clean the piss off your hands (hopefully, you're skilled enough NOT to piss on your hands). Instead, washing after pissing prevents other people from getting the coliform bacteria that lives in your pants. Urine is pretty sterile, and your dick doesn't get dirty packed in cotton all day. But it's those germs that are problematic, and your crotch provides a nice warm haven for them. You don't want to spread your bacteria to doorknobs and handshakes during the day. And you hope other guys aren't passing their crotch-fed bacteria to you during a handshake. So wash your hands with soap and water, or an antibacterial soap, after every trip to the can.

SPEED BEER

There are few activities on the planet that are as inherently male as drinking beer quickly with the sole purpose of getting fucked up. Women will drink beer, but not in massive quantities and not usually with the intent of downing several gallons in the course of a single evening.

Because beer comes in containers with only one opening, the speed with which you can ingest beer is limited by air flow and air pressure on the liquid. You can chug a beer, but only by breathing a lot of air back into the bottle or can while you're doing it. This results in a lot of foam and a throat/lung workout that detracts from the overall pleasure of the experience.

The way around the inherent drawback in beer bottles and cans is to add air pressure to the equation. This can be accomplished using two traditional methods: either by shooting a beer, or creating a beer funnel.

SHOOTING

Shooting a beer requires a can of beer and a can opener. The unopened can is turned upside down and a small puncture is made to the bottom using the can opener. Don't use a knife or screwdriver, unless you're incredibly desperate: they have a habit of slipping off the can and getting embedded deep in the flesh of your hand.

Once you've got a hole in the bottom of the can, keep it in that position and raise it up above your head. Tilting your head back, place the can's pull tab (which is now on the underside of the can) over your mouth. With your free hand, slip your index finger under the tab and pull down. This will release the beer with all the force of Category 5 toilet flush. Swallow as fast as you can, and don't try to breathe. Once it starts, there's no way to stop the flow. The beer should be completely drained in less than eight seconds, so you're not going to suffocate or choke if you do it right.

Keep in mind that the closer you hold the can to your mouth, the less beer you're going to be wearing.

FUNNELING

Funneling a beer requires, not surprisingly, a device called a beer funnel, also known as a beer bong. The principle behind a beer funnel is the same as that for shooting a beer, although you can get more beer in a funnel and have more control of the start and stop process.

The first step involves constructing a working device, which requires purchasing a large funnel that will hold at least 16 oz. of liquid—and preferably more. You can get these at hardware stores, the laundry section of the supermarket, or auto supply stores. Next, you have to attach tubing that fits tightly around the funnel spout. This can be any kind of clean tubing, from the Tygon tubing found in chemistry labs to the clear hoses used for large air pumps in aquariums. Again, large hardware stores are good sources.

Affix three feet of the tube to the funnel. This is your device in its most elemental state. Some enterprising funnelers add valves to control beer flow, but most drinkers use their fingers to regulate the liquid by pinching the tube at the appropriate time.

Funneling is a two-man job at the very minimum. If you are the drinker, then someone else needs to hold the funnel over your head, as high as possible. This can be accomplished by having him stand on a chair or on a stairway above you, or you can lay on the floor with him standing over you. Take the end of the tubing—the hanging part not connected to the funnel—and pinch the end closed with your fingers. For more dramatic effect, you can also seal it by sticking your tongue into it.

Your friend fills the funnel with the requisite amount

of beer from cans, bottles, or a keg. This may be more than the standard 16 oz. in a can or bottle, so you'll want to start by taking a deep breath. When you're ready, stop pinching the tube and let it flow. Again, the force is tremendous, aided by gravity, but unlike shooting a beer, you can pinch the tube shut or clamp it with your teeth to stop the flow.

Variations on beer funneling include multiple funnels feeding one tube for a variety of beer flavors, using a Y-connector, or drinking straight from the funnel without any tubing (typically a messy procedure).

As always, drinkers must be careful not to overdo funneling, as the human stomach can only hold about two quarts of liquid at a time. If more than that is shoved down your throat, your stomach may decide to force it back out—the same way it came in.

• •

HOW TO TIE A TIE

Let's face it. Ties suck. Sure, they look good on the right occasions, but they're tight, uncomfortable, and probably the only part of your wardrobe where you're never sure if it matches. Plus, fewer and fewer companies or events require them, so ties are going the way of Courtney Love's career.

Still, there are those occasions when you might actually have to knot one of these designer nooses. Here's the easiest tie to knot, called the four-in-hand, and it will do you fine no matter what the occasion. And screw learning to tie bow ties; the department store makes them pre-tied just fine. If you want to learn how to tie a Windsor, Half-Windsor, or a Pratt, go to finishing school.

The following illustrations are what you should see in a mirror:

1) Flip your shirt collar up and drape the tie around your neck. Start with the wide end of the tie on your right, extending about a foot below the skinny end.
2) Cross the wide end over the skinny side under your chin and back underneath.
3) Continue around the front, passing the wide end across the front of the skinny end once more. Now you've looped around the skinny side.
4) Pull the wide end up through the loop that you've made.
5) Hold the front of the knot loose with your index finger, and pull the wide end down this loop in front.

6) Remove finger and tighten knot carefully. Do this by holding the knot with your left hand and pulling down on the skinny end with your right hand. If the skinny end sticks out below the wide end, start over but extend the wide end a little more than before.

7) Draw up tight to your collar. Make sure you've buttoned your top shirt button, and make the knot snug up against your throat. Like a noose.

● ●

GREATEST DRUMMERS OF ALL TIME

Buddy Rich (jazz)

Keith Moon (rock)

John Bonham (rock)

Art Blakey (jazz)

Bill Bruford (rock, jazz)

Neal Peart (rock)

Carl Palmer (rock)

Tony Williams (jazz)

Gene Krupa (jazz)

Hal Blaine (studio drummer)

Billy Cobham (rock, jazz)

Ringo Starr (rock)

Terry Bozzio (rock)

GIRLS WHO PUT OUT

What would the world be like without those girls who jump in the backseat of our cars and drop their pants at the mere mention of the word "fuck"? For many guys, it would be a world where they get laid a loss less than they currently do.

Sluts, whores, tramps, skanks, and their fellow females are not to be confused with twats, cunts, and bitches. This latter group of girls are just females who piss you off. Generally, you would have no interest in fucking them because they're mean-spirited and downright conniving. They'd cut your balls off as soon as blow you. Think Hillary Clinton, think Rosie O'Donnell.

Sluts, whores, tramps, and skanks are sexual sisters of mercy, existing to make sure you get your rocks off. They come in all shapes and sizes, but their unifying characteristic—and inherent charm—is their ability to go down faster than the *Titanic*.

Here's the definitive guide to girls who put out.

Slut: will do anything you want for the sheer pleasure of it, no strings attached. She's selective, but not overly so, and is usually fun to be around even when she's not fucking. She wears underwear, and likes to find ways to flash it in public.

Whore: will sleep with you in exchange for something else, usually money, a meal, or a concert ticket. A whore will give it up to anyone. There is also a certain trashiness in a whore, like the way she shoves her breasts into a bra two sizes too small. Only wears underwear if she remembers where she left it.

Tramp: a whore who doesn't even bother to get something in exchange. Probably doesn't own any underwear.

Skank: a tramp with a venereal disease. If she has underwear, she doesn't wash it. You'll fuck her, but you better have a pack of condoms, all your shots, and a shower stall nearby.

Hooker: a professional whore. She'll fuck you nine ways from Sunday, but only if you have cash.

Prostitute: a classy hooker, but not by a whole lot.

Escort: an upscale prostitute who will fuck you for a lot of money after you've bought her a nice dinner and maybe taken her to the theater. In exchange, you get a good-looking babe who knows how to suck the chrome off a trailer hitch and still keep herself clean and discrete. She doesn't wear underwear; she wears lingerie.

COLOR CHEAT SHEET

At some point in your married (or cohabitational) life, you will come into contact with colors. Yeah, you think you know them all: blue, yellow, red, green, purple, orange, black, and white. Maybe a few others you remember from the big Crayola 64 box. Compared to your significant other, you don't know dick. It's an easy bet that your significant other will know upwards of sixteen thousand colors, many of which are created specifically by catalog merchandisers and paint manufacturers to mess you up—and give women something to agonize over. In reality, they're all a variation on the three primary (blue, yellow, red) and three complementary (green, purple, orange) colors.

The problem is that one day you're going to be asked your opinion about these colors. It may have to do with the color of shoes, window treatments, dresses, slips, couches, skirts, blouses, deck furniture, upholstery, kitchen countertops, and even random pieces of fabric that are mysteriously lying around your house— perhaps draped over the arm of a chair or sitting on a pillowcase. What makes it problematic is that you're going to be expected to know the names of these goddamned colors. Short of pulling every paint chip from Home Depot and every fabric swatch from Calico Corners, you are dead in the water because your lack of color knowledge will frustrate your significant other to the point of rage.

So we're going to try and help a little here. We've compiled a list of some of the most popular catalog colors and grouped them together. Take time to look these over. Learn them, perhaps memorize them. If need be, whip out this book at the store and do some quick cheatsheeting. This guide could save your wallet and your relationship—and maybe even your sanity.

NOTE: Pastels are an entirely different group of colors, as are neons. Pastels refer mostly to lighter shades of regular colors, but it would be way too easy to call them "lighter shades of some color." The best way to remember pastel colors is that they are the kind that guys would normally refer to as "wimpy" or "pussy" colors.

BLUE

Periwinkle • Wedgewood • Ultramarine • Cyan • Indigo • Ink • Lapis • Cornflower • French Blue • Royal • Navy • Cadet • Harbor • Bristol • Azure • Mediterranean

LIGHT BLUE

Chambray • Peacock • Sky • Newport

RED

Poppy • Henna • Aubergine • Sangria • Garnet • Bitter-sweet • Magenta • Berry • Cardinal • Cranberry • Rasp-berry • Scarlet • Brick

LIGHT RED

Watermelon

YELLOW

Honey • Plantain • Daffodil • Sunburst • Maize • Gold • Chamois • Butter • Buttercup • Sumac

GREEN-BLUE

Lagoon • Turquoise • Pond • Jade • Teal

GREEN

Hunter • Kelly • Moss • Loden • Forest • Parsley • Spruce • Clover • Fern

LIGHT GREEN

Pistachio • Lime • Sage • Glacier • Frosty Mint • Sea Foam

ORANGE

Persimmon • Tangerine • Terracota • Melon • Pumpkin • Coral • Mango • Ochre

LIGHT ORANGE

Apricot • Peach

PURPLE

Grape • Plum • Eggplant • Imperial Purple • Bordeaux • Amethyst

LIGHT PURPLE

Lilac • Lavender • Hyacinth • Dusty Violet

BROWN

Caramel • Russet • Smoke • Camel • Mocha • Coffee • Cocoa • Chestnut • Spice • Muted Olive • Pinecone

LIGHT BROWN

Mushroom • Khaki • Bronze • Tan • Cognac • Sand • Cappucino • Hemp • Taupe

GRAY

Stone • Heather • Charcoal • Clay • Zinc • Granite • Pewter • Slate • Steel •

PINK

Antique Rose • Blush • Shrimp

BEIGE/CREAM/OFF-WHITE (ALL HAVE A TOUCH OF GRAY OR BROWN)

• Llama • Parchment • Eggshell • Oyster • Balsam • Chalk • Vanilla • Opal • Pearl • Ivory • Cream • Pebble • Oatmeal • Papyrus • Wheat • Putty • Ecru • Navajo

COLOR WITHOUT DEFINITION AND WHICH IS NOT FOUND IN NATURE

Chartreuse (kind of muddy lime-green)

Some rules of thumb for remembering colors if you're ever in a bind (or in a department store):

- If it resembles any kind of mineral or ore, it is probably a shade of gray (pewter, zinc, steel, etc.).
- If it begins with a "C", it is probably some shade of brown (caramel, camel, cappucino, chestnut, etc.).
- If it sounds like something you can eat, it is probably brown, unless it is some kind of fruit normally associated with breakfast cereals, like strawberries or raspberries. In that case, it's probably red.
- If it's something organic that you can refer to by a scent, it is probably a form of purple.
- If you stroll through it, or roll around in it, it's a green (forest, spruce, moss, etc.).

A COLLECTION OF THOUGHTS ON SEX AND LOVE

Virginity can be cured.

Sex is a three-letter word which needs some old-fashioned four-letter words to convey its full meaning.

There may be some things better than sex and some things worse than sex. But there is nothing exactly like it.

There is no remedy for sex but more sex.

Never sleep with anyone crazier than yourself.

A woman never forgets the men she could have had; a man never forgets the women he couldn't.

There is no difference between a wise man and a fool when they fall in love.

Nothing improves with age.

The more beautiful the woman is who loves you, the easier it is to leave her with no hard feelings.

No matter how many times you've had it, if it's offered take it, because it'll never be quite the same again.

Sex has no calories.

Sex takes up the least amount of time and causes the most amount of trouble.

Love is the triumph of imagination over intelligence.

Sex appeal is 50 percent what you've got and 50 percent what people think you've got.

The qualities that most attract a woman to a man are usually the same ones she can't stand years later.

Sex is dirty only if it's done right.

When the lights are out, all women are beautiful.

Sex is hereditary. If your parents never had it, chances are you won't either.

Sow your wild oats on Saturday night, and on Sunday pray for crop failure.

The game of love is never called off on account of darkness.

It was not the apple on the tree but the pair on the ground that caused the trouble in the garden.

Sex discriminates against the shy and the ugly.

Love your neighbor, but don't get caught.

If the effort that went into research on the female bosom had gone into our space program, we would now be running hot dog stands on the moon.

Love is a matter of chemistry, sex is a matter of physics.

One good turn gets most of the blankets.

It is better to have loved and lost than never to have loved at all.

Never lie down with a woman who's got more troubles than you.

What matters is not the length of the wand, but the magic in the stick.

It is better to be looked over than overlooked.

Never say no.

A man can be happy with any woman as long as he doesn't love her.

Beauty is skin deep; ugly is to the bone.

Never argue with a woman when she's tired—or rested.

Love comes in spurts.

Sex is one of the nine reasons for reincarnation; the other eight are unimportant.

Love is the delusion that one woman differs from another.

"This won't hurt, I promise."

WRITERS EVERY GUY SHOULD READ

It's hard to get anyone to read anymore, let alone admit that they own books. To be well rounded, you should own at least one book by each of the following guy authors. And read them.

Sir Arthur Conan Doyle: *The Speckled Band, The Hound of the Baskervilles*

Ernest Hemingway: *For Whom the Bell Tolls, The Old Man and the Sea*

Mark Twain: *Adventures of Huckleberry Finn, The Mysterious Stranger*

Edgar Allan Poe: *The Black Cat, The Tell-Tale Heart, The Fall of the House of Usher*

Stephen King: *Carrie, The Shining, The Stand*

Tom Clancy: *The Hunt for Red October, Clear and Present Danger*

John Grisham: *The Client, A Time to Kill*

Isaac Asimov: The *Foundation* Trilogy

Louis L'Amour: *Lando, The Sackett Brand*

Kurt Vonnegut: *Cat's Cradle, Slaughterhouse Five*

John Steinbeck: *Cannery Row, The Grapes of Wrath*

Ray Bradbury: *The Illustrated Man, Something Wicked this Way Comes*

Dave Barry: *Dave Barry Turns 40, The World According to Dave Barry*

Sophocles: *Oedipus the King, Electra*

William Faulkner: *The Sound and the Fury, The Unvanguished*

Elmore Leonard: *Get Shorty, Glitz*
George Orwell: *1984, Animal Farm*
William Shakespeare: *everything, except the sonnets*

· ·

THOSE NAMES WE CAN NEVER REMEMBER

THE TWELVE APOSTLES

Simon, Andrew, James, John, Philip, Bartholomew, Thomas, Matthew, James son of Alphaeus, Jude, Simon the Zealot, Judas Iscariot

SANTA'S REINDEER

Dasher, Dancer, Prancer, Vixen, Comet, Cupid, Donner, Blitzen. Later joined by Rudolph.

THE SEVEN DWARVES

Bashful, Doc, Dopey, Grumpy, Happy, Sleepy, Sneezy

THE THREE WISE MEN

Balthasar, Gaspar, Melchior

THE THREE MUSKETEERS

Athos, Porthos, Aramis. Joined by D'Artagnan.

THE JACKSON FIVE

Jackie (Sigmund Esco), Tito (Tariano Adaryll), Jermaine (Jermaine La Juane), Marlon (Marlon David), Michael (Michael Joseph). Randy (Steven Randall) joined later.
Sisters: Rebbie (Maureen Reilette), La Toya Yvonne, Janet Damita Jo

THE THREE PHILOSOPHERS

Socrates, Plato, Aristotle

THE MARX BROTHERS

Groucho, Chico, Harpo, Zeppo, Gummo

THE THREE STOOGES

Moe (Howard), Larry (Fine), Curly (Howard), Shemp (Howard), Joe (Besser), Curly Joe (DeRita)

THE FOUR HORSEMEN OF THE APOCALYPSE

War, Famine, Pestilence, Death

JAMES BOND ACTORS

Sean Connery, George Lazenby, Roger Moore, Timothy Dalton, Pierce Brosnan, Daniel Craig

DEATH AS A CAREER MOVE

Most guys think being a rock star would be the coolest job in the world. Interestingly, a few people disagree. In fact, some of these people are rock stars. They can't handle the job, or just don't want to. Below are a list of people who apparently felt that taking a dirt nap was better than being a famous musician. You know, it's one thing to die in a plane crash or get killed on a motorcycle, but going out on your own dime is, plain and simple, a waste.

Kurt Cobain, Nirvana: gunshot wound, self-inflicted

Jimi Hendrix: choked on own vomit

John Bonham, Led Zeppelin: choked on own vomit

Keith Moon, The Who: overdose of alcoholism medicine

John Entwistle, The Who: heart attack brought on by cocaine use (if anybody should have known better, Entwistle should have)

Michael Hutchence, INXS: suicide by hanging (possibly autoerotic asphyxiation)

Hillel Slovak, Red Hot Chili Peppers: heroin overdose

Steve Clark, Def Leppard: alcoholism

James Honeyman-Scott, The Pretenders: heroin overdose

Pete Farndon, The Pretenders: heroin overdose

Sid Vicious, Sex Pistols: heroin overdose

Doug Hopkins, Gin Blossoms: handgun blast, self-inflicted

Roy Buchanan: suicide by hanging

Lowell George, Little Feat: drug overdose

Mike Bloomfield, Butterfield Blues Band: drug overdose

Paul Butterfield, Butterfield Blues Band: alcohol
Jimmy McCulloch, Wings: drug-induced heart failure
Tommy Bolin, Deep Purple: drug overdose
Paul Kossoff, Free: drug-induced heart failure
Peter Ham, Badfinger: suicide by hanging
Tom Evans, Badfinger: suicide by hanging
Layne Staley, Alice in Chains: heroin overdose
Jonathan Melvoin, Smashing Pumpkins: heroin over-
  dose
Andrew Wood, Mother Love Bone: heroin overdose
Brian Cole, The Association: heroin overdose
Shannon Hoon, Blind Melon: drug overdose
Richard Manuel, The Band: suicide by hanging
Bon Scott, AC/DC: alcohol overdose
Johnny Thunder, New York Dolls: heroin overdose
Dee Dee Ramone, The Ramones: heroin overdose
Gary Thain, Uriah Heep: heroin overdose
Bob Stinson, The Replacements: drug overdose
John Panozzo, Styx: alcoholism
Stuart Adamson, Big Country: suicide by hanging

• •

THINGS NEVER TO SAY TO YOUR WIFE

About her hair *after* she's been to the salon:

"You're kidding. They charged you for that?"
"Did they give you a hat to go with it?"
"Is that what you really wanted it to look like?"

"Don't worry. No one will notice."
"I liked it better before."

About other women:

"Oh man, look at the tits on her!"
"Babe alert at two o'clock."
"You should do your hair like hers."
"God, your sister is hot."
"I wouldn't call her the 'other woman.' She's only fourteen."

About her pregnancy:

"Well, couldn't they induce labor? The twenty-first is the
    Super Bowl."
"Not to imply anything, but I don't think the kid weighs
    thirty pounds."
"I sure hope your thighs aren't going to stay that flabby
    forever."
"I know you're eating for two, but geez . . . it's a tiny
    baby, not Chris Farley."
"Maybe we should name the baby after my secretary,
    Brandi."

About her weight:

"You're right, it does make you look fat."
"Honey, it just means there's tons more of you to love."
"Happy Birthday! It's something I know you really
    need—a membership to the gym."
"All that extra weight looks good on you. At least now I
    can see your tits."

"Wow. Was there a special on cellulite?"

"Yeah, those pants do make your butt look big. But isn't
  that the look you're going for?"

- -

ESSENTIAL GUY ALBUMS

There are certain albums you should have in your collection to be considered a complete guy. Any guy, no matter
how old or young, will find something to like in here.
Most of them are rock, but there are a few other styles
represented. You may not have one or two of the following, that's acceptable. But if you're missing three or
more, you've got some serious catching up to do.

AC/DC: *Back in Black*
Aerosmith: *Toys in the Attic*
The Allman Brothers: *At Fillmore East (Live)*
The Beatles: *Abbey Road, Revolver,* at least one compilation
Black Sabbath: *Paranoid*
David Bowie: *Ziggy Stardust and the Spiders from Mars*
Johnny Cash: *At San Quentin* or *At Folsom Prison*
The Clash: *London Calling*
Cream: *The Very Best of Cream*
Miles Davis: *Kind of Blue* or *Bitches' Brew*
Deep Purple: *Machine Head*
Jimi Hendrix: *Smash Hits*
Robert Johnson: *The Robert Johnson Collection*
Led Zeppelin: *Led Zeppelin II* and the fourth album
Lynyrd Skynyrd: *Pronounced*

Metallica: Black Album

Nirvana: *Nevermind*

Pink Floyd: *Dark Side of the Moon*

Elvis Presley: Elv1s 30 #1 Hits

The Rolling Stones: *Hot Rocks, Sticky Fingers*, or *Exile on Main Street*

Frank Sinatra: *Reprise: The Very Good Years*

Soundgarden: *Superunknown*

Bruce Springsteen: *Born to Run*

U2: *War*

Van Halen: *Van Halen*

Stevie Ray Vaughan & Double Trouble: *Greatest Hits*

The Who: *Who's Next*

Neil Young: *Decade*

There are no opera records here. None. Guys don't do opera.

• •

INFAMOUS AMERICAN MURDERERS

And you thought your college roommate was a weirdo.

Jeffrey Dahmer: The guy who would eat anything, hacked up and ate his victims, killed seventeen.

Richard Ramirez: The Night Stalker and avowed Satanist, killed sixteen. This loser was caught by neighbors who chased him down the street and beat him.

Ted Bundy: A guy who killed the prettiest women he

could find—between twenty and forty of them. What a dick.

John Wayne Gacy: Part-time kiddie clown and general contractor who insulated his basement with the bodies of thirty-three young men.

Albert DeSalvo: The Boston Strangler, represented by F. Lee Bailey, making F. Lee famous well before the O. J. Simpson trial. DeSalvo killed thirteen, usually while maintaining a hard-on.

Charles Manson: Whack-job who thought the Beatles were warning him about Armageddon, so he and his "family" killed nine people in and around L.A.

Charles Starkweather: At only five feet two inches, the original rebel without a clue had a lot of issues. So he took his fourteen-year-old girlfriend and went on a multi-state killing spree, murdering eleven.

Henry Lee Lucas: The ultimate loser/drifter claimed to have killed more than a hundred people, starting with his mother.

Charles Whitman: Couldn't take the constant nagging from his wife and mother, so he killed them. Then he climbed a Texas clock tower with his high-powered rifle and killed sixteen more.

Wayne Williams: A black guy who killed twenty-eight black boys in and around Atlanta.

Angelo Buono and Kenneth Bianchi: The Hillside Stranglers, cousins who had a thing for little girls, killed ten.

Richard Speck: A perennial loser who couldn't get a decent date, so he killed eight nurses all in one night in one apartment.

Leonard Lake and Charles Ng: Created a death cabin and

tortured anyone they could find, including babies, and videotaped it all. Killed as many as twenty-five.

Edmund Kemper: The Gentle Giant killed ten hitchhikers and old ladies, starting with his grandparents, and then his mom, whose skull he used for masturbatory purposes.

Lawrence Bittaker and Roy Norris: Prison rejects who constructed a torture van to kill pretty girls. Convicted of five murders, but thought to have killed dozens more.

H. H. Holmes (Herman Mudgett): Created the human version of the "roach hotel" ("Guests check in but they never check out!") during Chicago's World's Fair. Killed as many as two hundred of his tenants.

Gary Leon Ridgeway: Set a modern-day record for serial killing, pleading guilty to the murders of forty-eight women, mostly runaways and prostitutes. Known as the Green River Killer, he told police he "thought he was doing them a favor" by getting the hookers off the street.

● ●

CONVERSION: TEMPERATURE

Do the following to change a Celsius temperature quickly into Fahrenheit: Take the Celsius reading—say, 10 degrees C—then double it and add 32. That gives you 10+10+32, or 52 degrees Farenheit. Pretty damn close.

Once you get into higher numbers, tack on two or three degrees to get even closer.

If you want to go from Fahrenheit to Celsius, do it this way: take the Fahrenheit reading—say 80 degrees F—and subtract 32. Now you've got 48. Cut that in half and you have 24. That's your temperature in Celsius. (FYI, for most purposes, Celsius and centigrade are interchangeable terms: Celsius is the guy who invented it, centigrade is the form of measurement.)

Don't worry about transferring to Kelvin, which is based on absolute zero, or 459 degrees F below zero. If you're trying to figure out temperatures in Kelvin, you're either in a lab or already dead.

• •

BEER ALCOHOL CONTENT

DOMESTIC BEERS

BRAND	BREWERY	% ALCOHOL
Anchor Porter	Anchor	5.66
Anchor Steam	Anchor	4.63
Anheuser-Busch Natural Light	Anheuser-Busch	4.12
Ballantine Private Stock Malt Liquor	Narragansett	6.01
Ballantine Premium Lager	Falstaff	4.82
Blatz Beer	G. Heileman	4.86

BRAND	BREWERY	% ALCOHOL
Blatz Milwaukee 1851 Beer	Blatz	4.48
Bud Light	Anheuser-Busch	3.88
Budweiser	Anheuser-Busch	4.82
Busch Beer	Anheuser-Busch	5.19
Carling Black Label	G. Heileman	4.38
Colt45 Malt Liquor	G. Heileman	6.11
Coors Banquet Beer	Adolph Coors	5.03
Coors Light	Adolph Coors	4.36
Genesee 12 Horse Ale	Genesee	4.98
Genesee Beer	Genesee	5.03
Genesee Cream Ale	Genesee	4.70
Genesee Light Beer	Genesee	3.55
George Killian's Irish Red Ale	Adolph Coors	5.79
George Killian's Irish Red Brand Beer	Adolph Coors	5.54
Hamm's Beer	Pabst	4.53
Lowenbrau Dark	Miller	5.00
Lowenbrau Special Beer	Miller	5.12
Michelob Beer	Anheuser-Busch	4.99
Michelob Classic Dark	Anheuser-Busch	4.76
Michelob Light	Anheuser-Busch	4.52
Mickey's Fine Malt Liquor	G. Heileman	5.70

BRAND	BREWERY	% ALCOHOL
Miller Genuine Draft	Miller	5.02
Miller High Life	Miller	4.80
Miller Lite	Miller	4.40
Old Milwaukee Light	Stroh	3.82
Old Milwaukee Beer	Stroh	4.51
Olde English 800 Malt Liquor	Pabst	6.13
Olympia Premium Lager	Pabst	4.78
Pabst Blue Ribbon	Pabst	5.01
Pabst Extra Light Low Alcohol	Pabst	2.50
Red White & Blue	G. Heileman	5.15
Rolling Rock Extra Pale	Latrobe	4.64
Rolling Rock Premium Beer	Latrobe	4.51
Sam Adams Boston Lager	Boston Beer	4.88
Schaefer Beer	Stroh	4.66
Schlitz Beer	Stroh	4.70
Schlitz Light	Stroh	4.28
Schlitz Malt Liquor	Stroh	6.29
Sierra Nevada Pale Ale	Sierra Nevada	4.82
Sierra Nevada Porter	Sierra Nevada	5.34

BRAND	BREWERY	% ALCOHOL
Sierra Nevada Stout	Sierra Nevada	5.10
Signature Stroh Beer	Stroh	4.84
Stroh's Beer	Stroh	4.68
Stroh's Light	Stroh	4.45
Tuborg Deluxe Dark Export	G. Heileman	5.11
Tuborg Export Quality	G. Heileman	5.02
Yuengling Porter D.G.	Yuengling & Son (USA)	4.13
Yuengling Premium Beer D.G.	Yuengling & Son (USA)	4.65

IMPORTED BEERS

BRAND	BREWER (COUNTRY)	% ALCOHOL
Amstel Light	Amstel Brouwerij B.V. (Holland)	3.96
Asahi Draft Beer	Asahi (Japan)	5.21
Bass & Co.'s Pale Ale	Bass (England)	5.51
Beamish Irish Cream Stout	BeamishCrawford (Ireland)	4.95
Beck's Beer	Brauerei Beck (Germany)	5.13
Cerveza Carta Blanca	Cerveceria Cuauhtémoc (Mexico)	4.02
Cerveza Tecate Beer	Cerveceria Cuauhtémoc (Mexico)	4.49

BRAND	BREWER (COUNTRY)	% ALCOHOL
Chester Golden Ale	Greenall Whitley (England)	5.43
Corona Extra Beer	Cereveria Modela SA (Mexico)	4.84
Dos Equis XX Imported Beer	Cuauhtémoc (Mexico)	4.79
Dos Equis XX Special Lager	Cerveceria Moctezuma (Mexico)	4.96
Dragon Stout	Desnoes—Geddes (Jamaica)	6.79
Foster's Lager	Carlton & United (Australia)	5.25
Fürstenberg German Beer	Fürstlich Fürstenbergische (Germany)	4.43
Great Wall	Green Bamboo (China)	4.63
Greenall's Cheshire English Pub Beer	Greenall Whitley PLC (England)	5.00
Grizzly Canadian Lager	Hamilton (Canada)	5.4
Grolsch Lager Beer	Grolsch Bierbrouwerij (Holland)	5.17
Guinness Extra Stout	Guinness (Ireland)	4.27
Harp	Harp (Ireland)	4.55
Heineken Lager Beer	Heineken (Holland)	5.41

BRAND	BREWER (COUNTRY)	% ALCOHOL
Heineken Special Dark Beer	Heineken (Holland)	5.17
Kirin Beer	Kirin (Japan)	6.85
Kronenbourg Beer	Kronenbourg (France)	5.11
Kronenbourg Imported Dark Beer	Kronenbourg (France)	5.08
Labatt's 50	Labatt's (Canada)	5.34
McEwan's Scotch Ale	Scottish & Newcastle (Scotland)	9.50
Molson Canadian Beer	Molson (Canada)	5.19
Molson Golden Beer	Molson (Canada)	6.04
Molson Light	Molson (Canada)	2.41
Moosehead Canadian Lager Beer	Moosehead (Canada)	5.08
Nordik Wolf Light	A.B. Pripps Bryggerier (Sweden)	4.70
O'Keefe Canadian Beer	O'Keefe (Canada)	4.96
Pilsner Urquell Beer	Pilsner Urquell Pilsen (Czech Republic)	4.25

BRAND	BREWER (COUNTRY)	% ALCOHOL
Red Stripe Lager Beer	Desnoes & Geddes (Jamaica)	5.04
Sheaf Stout	Carlton & United (Australia)	5.28
Sol Cerveza Especial	Cerveceria Moctezuma (Mexico)	4.13
Spaten Munich Special Dark Beer	Spaten-Brau (Germany)	6.63
St. Pauli Girl Beer	St. Pauli (Germany)	5.00
St. Pauli Girl Dark Beer	St. Pauli (Germany)	5.02
Suntory Draft Beer	Suntory (Japan)	4.64
Superior Imported Beer	Cerveceria Moctezuma (Mexico)	4.34
Thos Cooper & Sons Adelaide Lager	Cooper & Sons (Australia)	4.27
Thos Cooper & Sons Real Ale	Cooper & Sons (Australia)	6.77
Thos Cooper & Sons Stout	Cooper & Sons (Australia)	7.10
Tolly Original Premium Ale	Tollemache & Cobbold (England)	4.85
Tsingtao Beer	Tsingtao (China)	4.79

BRAND	BREWER (COUNTRY)	% ALCOHOL
Watney's Red Barrel Beer	Stag (England)	3.92
Würzburger Hofbräu	Würtzburger Hofbräu AG (Germany)	5.42
Würtzburger Hofbräu Light	Würtzburger Hofbräu AG (Germany)	5.44

• •

TOP BEER DRINKING COUNTRIES

Beer is the universal alcoholic beverage. Nearly every culture on the planet has figured out how to create beer. Some countries party harder than others when it comes to sucking the suds. The numbers below indicate how many gallons the people of each country consume on average over the course of a year. The number is spread over the total population, so if you eliminate the women and children, some guys must be drinking the beer equivalent of a tanker truck.

1) Czech Republic   42
2) Ireland   35
3) Germany   31
4) Australia   29
5) Austria   28
6) United Kingdom   26

7)	Belgium	25
8)	Denmark	24
9)	Finland	23
10)	Luxembourg	22
11)	Slovakia	22
12)	Spain	22
13)	United States	22
14)	Croatia	21
15)	Netherlands	20

Americans drink about 235 bottles of beer every year. The Czechs drink nearly double that amount, pretty much because there's nothing else to do.

• •

TOP BEER BRANDS WORLDWIDE

1)	Budweiser	Anheuser-Busch
2)	Bud Light	Anheuser-Busch
3)	Skol	InBev
4)	Asahi Super Dry	Asahi Breweries Ltd.
5)	Corona Extra	Grupo Modelo
6)	Heineken	Heineken NV
7)	Coors Light	Molson Coors Brewing
8)	Brahma Chopp	InBev
9)	Miller Lite	SABMiller
10)	Polar	Cerveceria Polar CA
11)	Castle Lager	SABMiller
12)	Kaiser	Cervejarias Kaiser

13) Amstel   Heineken NV
14) Kirin Lager   Kirin Brewery
15) Antartica Pilsen   InBev
16) Carlsberg   Carlsberg A/S
17) San Miguel Pale Pilsen   San Miguel Corp.
18) Guinness Stout   Guinness Brewing
    Worldwide
19) Natural Light   Anheuser-Busch
20) Aguila   Bavaria SA

WORLD'S BIGGEST BREWERS

InBev	Belgium
SABMiller	U.K.
Anheuser-Busch	U.S.
Heineken NV	Netherlands
Carlsberg Breweries A/S	Denmark
Scottish Courage	U.K.
Grupo Modelo	Mexico
Molson Coors Brewing	Canada
Baltic Beverages Holding	Russia
Tsingtao Brewery	China

WORDS OF WISDOM: DRINKING

Cliff Clavin (postal worker, *Cheers*) on the importance of drinking and thinking.

"Well, ya see, it's like this. A herd of buffalo can only move as fast as the slowest buffalo. And when the herd is hunted, it is the slowest and weakest ones at the back that are killed first. This natural selection is good for the herd as a whole, because the general speed and health of the whole group keeps improving by the regular killing of the weakest members.

"In much the same way, the human brain can only operate as fast as the slowest brain cells. Excessive intake of alcohol, as we know, kills brain cells. But naturally, it attacks the slowest and weakest brain cells first. In this way, regular consumption of beer eliminates the weaker brain cells, making the brain a faster and more efficient machine. That's why you always feel smarter after a few beers."

CONDOMS

Cover your stump before you hump.
The right selection is to protect your erection.
Wrap it in foil before checking her oil.
A crank with armor will never harm her.

If you really love her, wear a cover.

Don't make a mistake, cover your snake.

Before you attack her, wrap your whacker.

Don't be silly, protect your willy.

When in doubt, shroud your spout.

Don't be a loner, cover your boner.

You can't go wrong if you shield your dong.

If you're not going to sack it, go home and whack it.

If you think she's spunky, cover your monkey.

If you slip between her thighs, condomize.

It will be sweeter if you wrap your peter.

She won't get sick if you wrap your dick.

If you go into heat, package your meat.

While you're undressing Venus, dress up your penis.

When you take off her pants and blouse, suit up your mouse.

Especially in December, gift wrap your member.

Never ever deck her with an unwrapped pecker.

Don't be a fool, vulcanize your tool.

Sex is cleaner with a packaged wiener.

If you can't shield your rocket, leave it in your pocket.

No glove, no love.

• •

FLY-FISHING

10 o'clock—position of forward cast

2 o'clock—position of back cast

12 o'clock—straight up

BASIC EQUIPMENT:

Rod: A five weight, 8½ or 9 foot, three- or four-piece travel rod

Reel: a single action, should hold 100 yards of backing and floating fly line

Line: weight forward, five weight floating line

Leader: 4X, 5X, and 6X leaders, minimum 7 to 9 foot

Tippet: roll of fluorocarbon 5X and 6X for tying on flies

Flies: Dry: Adams, size 14, 16, and 18.
  Dry: Elk Hair Caddis, size 14, 16, and 18.
  Nymphs: size 14, 16, and 18.
  Black Woolly Buggers: size 10, 12.

Accessories: a fly-fishing vest with pockets, a hat, fly box, a pair of nippers, small forceps, sunscreen, insect repellant

Waders: depends on water temperature and depth. Available in neoprene, Gore-Tex, etc. Shallow fishing can be done with tennis shoes and shorts.

• •

PRIMARY TYPES OF FLIES

mayflies • caddis flies • stoneflies • midges • scuds and sowbugs • damsels and dragons • terrestrials • artificial flies

HOW TO MATCH THE ROD AND LINE WEIGHT TO THE FLY SIZE

ROD/LINE WEIGHT	FLY SIZES
3	12–28
4	10–26
5	8–24
6	6–20
7	4–16
8	1/0–12
9	2/0–10
10	3/0–8
11	4/0–6
12	6/0–4

• •

WORDS OF WISDOM: DAUGHTERS

At some point, most men will have daughters. This will be a source of joy, until those daughters realize that other men exist. It will be painful for you, but there is a way to prepare yourself upon the birth of your daughter(s), as outlined below.

First, buy a changing table that has drawers in it. Preferably made of heavy wood. Now, every time you finish changing your little angel on that diaper table, perform the following ritual. Drop your own testicles gently into the drawer while it is wide open. Then, giving yourself a lot of leverage, grab one edge of the drawer. With as much strength as you can muster, and with as much speed, slam the drawer shut as hard and as fast as you can. Make sure that your balls are smashed to the point of highest pain as the drawer closes. The pain you will feel will give you a hint, a mere hint, of the pain you will feel when your daughter grows up and starts dating some guy you know is little more than Mr. Penis.

• •

THE MOST ANNOYING WOMEN IN HISTORY

Barbra Streisand
Whoopi Goldberg
Hillary Rodham Clinton
Madonna
Rosanne Barr
Joan Rivers
Cher
Martha Stewart
Carrie Nation (crusaded against drinking, leading to Prohibition)

Notice that most of these women have been known at some point in their lives simply by their first names. There's a clue for you.

THE APPLE PIPE

For connoisseurs of the smoking arts, no predicament is as dire as finding yourself in possession of fine dried leaf and not having anything with which to smoke it. Or let's say you're the kind of smoker who doesn't want your smoking equipment to attract attention, especially when you're crossing international borders. In both cases, you might ask, "What's a smoker to do?"

The answer is simple. Make an apple pipe. Using a garden variety apple, you can smoke everything from dried pencil shavings and oregano to Sir Walter Raleigh's choicest tobacco and anything else you can imagine. The process is simple and can be done in less than a minute.

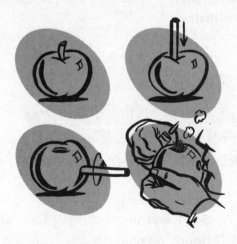

The indentation where the apple stem is will be your bowl. Pull the stem out and, using a small knife or pen, jam a hole about two-thirds of the way into the apple. Do this slightly off-center, so you don't have to drive through the core, but don't go all the way through the apple. If you're using a pen, stab it in once. If you have a thin knife blade, do it three times to open up more of the apple. Then scoop out a small portion of the apple around the indentation. Your bowl is complete.

Turn the apple sideways and repeat the stabbing procedure to create another hole where you will put your mouth. The two holes should now meet up in the middle of the apple at about a 90-degree angle. For truly enterprising pipe aficionados, drill a third hole diagonally into the apple from the opposite side of the mouthpiece. This can serve as a dedicated carb that regulates air flow, and you can open and close it with your finger.

When all the holes are in place, stuff the stuff you have into the bowl, light it up, and puff away. If whatever you're smoking makes you hungry, you can eat the apple when you're finished.

• •

SPORTS ILLUSTRATED SWIMSUIT ISSUE COVER MODELS

1964	Babette March
1965	Sue Peterson
1966	Sunny Bippus
1967	Marilyn Tindall
1968	Turia Mau
1969	Jamee Becker
1970	Cheryl Tiegs

1971	Tannia Rubiano
1972	Sheila Roscoe
1973	Dayle Haddon
1974	Ann Simonton
1975	Cheryl Tiegs
1976	Yvette and Yvonne Sylvander
1977	Lena Kansbod
1978	Maria Joao
1979	Christie Brinkley
1980	Christie Brinkley
1981	Christie Brinkley
1982	Carol Alt
1983	Cheryl Tiegs
1984	Paulina Porizkova
1985	Paulina Porizkova
1986	Elle Macpherson
1987	Elle Macpherson
1988	Elle Macpherson
1989	Kathy Ireland
1990	Judit Masco
1991	Ashley Montana Richardson
1992	Kathy Ireland
1993	Vendela Kirsebom
1994	Elle Macpherson, Kathy Ireland, Rachel Hunter
1995	Daniela Pestova
1996	Tyra Banks and Valeria Mazza
1997	Tyra Banks
1998	Heidi Klum
1999	Rebecca Romijn (Stamos)
2000	Daniela Pestova
2001	Elsa Benitez

2002	Yamila Diaz-Rahi
2003	Petra Němcová
2004	Veronica Vařeková
2005	Carolyn Murphy
2006	All Star SI Cover Models
2007	Beyoncé Knowles

• •

IN-YOUR-DREAMS CARS

If you can't get laid in one of these, you're a eunuch.

MODEL	HORSEPOWER AND PRICE TAG
Bugatti Veyron	1001 HP—$1.4 million
Lamborghini Reventon	650 HP—$1.4 million
Koenigsegg CCX	806 HP—$750,000
Pagani Zonda	650 HP—$690,000
SSC Ultimate Aero	1046 HP—$660,000
Leblanc Mirabeau	700 HP—$650,000
Ferrari Enzo	650 HP—$620,000
Saleen S7	750 HP—$550,000
Mercedes McLaren SLR	628 HP—$460,000
Rolls Royce Phantom Drophead Coupe	453 HP—$410,000
Mayback 62 Sedan	612 HP—$390,000
Spyker C12 La Turbie	500 HP—$350,000
Bentley Brooklands Coupe	530 HP—$350,000
Lamborghini Murciélago	640 HP—$320,000
Aston Martin DBS	520 HP—$270,000

THE WOMEN'S PERSPECTIVE

Women, by and large, have a limited sense of humor. It's not their fault; it's genetic. Women do not understand bathroom humor, sexual innuendo, or double entendres. They especially don't get practical jokes. They don't do them, they don't understand them. So keep them just between the guys.

Occasionally, they do manage to "make a funny" like the following list developed by an anonymous female. It's composed of hypothetical book titles that women think men should read. Read it. Laugh. Learn.

Combating Stupidity
You Can Do Housework, Too
PMS—Learning When to Keep Your Mouth Shut
How to Fill an Ice Cube Tray
We Do Not Want Sleazy Underthings for Christmas: Give Us Money
Wonderful Laundry Techniques (formerly *Don't Wash My Silks*)
Understanding the Female Response to Your Coming in Drunk at 4 A.M.
Parenting—It Doesn't End with Conception
Get a Life—Learn to Cook
How Not to Act Like an Asshole When You're Obviously Wrong
Spelling—Even You Can Get It Right
Underestimating Your Financial Incompetence
You—The Weaker Sex

Reasons to Give Flowers
How to Stay Awake After Sex
Why It Is Unacceptable to Relieve Yourself Anywhere but the Washroom
Garbage—Getting It to the Curb
#101 You Can Fall Asleep Without It If You Really Try
#201 The Morning Dilemma: If It's Awake, Take a Shower
Overcoming the "I'll Wear It If I Damn Well Please" Response
How to Put the Toilet Seat Down (formerly No, It Isn't a Bidet)
"The Weekend" and "Sports"—Not Synonyms!
Give Me a Break: Why We Know Your Excuses Are Bullshit
How to Go Shopping with Your Mate and Not Get Lost
The Remote Control: Overcoming Your Dependency
Romanticism—Other Ideas Besides Sex
Helpful Posture Hints for Couch Potatoes
Mothers-in-Law—They Are People, Too
How Not to Act Younger Than Your Children
You Too Can Be a Designated Driver
Male Bonding—Leave Your Friends at Home
Honest, You Don't Look Like Mel Gibson (Especially When You Are Naked)
Changing Your Underwear—It Really "Works"
The Attainable Goal—Omitting @#$%$#@
Fluffing the Blankets After Farting Is Not Necessary

STANLEY CUP CHAMPIONS

Hockey championships have been around since 1893. In 1892, Lord Stanley, Governor General of Canada, bought a $50 silver cup—called the Dominion Hockey Challenge Cup—to be given to the winner of an annual competition. The NHL was founded in 1917 and the cup was renamed the Stanley Cup. The seven-game series began in 1937.

YEAR	CHAMPIONSHIPS	FINAL ROUND OPPONENT	GAMES
2007	Anaheim Ducks	Ottawa Senators	4–1
2006	Carolina Hurricanes	Edmonton Oilers	4–3
2005	Not Held, season cancelled		
2004	Tampa Bay Lightning	Calgary Flames	4–3
2003	New Jersey Devils	Anaheim Mighty Ducks	4–3
2002	Detroit Red Wings	Carolina Hurricanes	4–1
2001	Colorado Avalanche	New Jersey Devils	4–3
2000	New Jersey Devils	Dallas Stars	4–2

YEAR	CHAMPIONSHIPS	FINAL ROUND OPPONENT	GAMES
1999	Dallas Stars	Buffalo Sabres	4–2
1998	Detroit Red Wings	Washington Capitals	4–0
1997	Detroit Red Wings	Philadelphia Flyers	4–0
1996	Colorado Avalanche	Florida Panthers	4–0
1995	New Jersey Devils	Detroit Red Wings	4–0
1994	New York Rangers	Vancouver Canucks	4–3
1993	Montreal Canadiens	Los Angeles Kings	4–1
1992	Pittsburgh Penguins	Chicago Black Hawks	4–0
1991	Pittsburgh Penguins	Minnesota North Stars	4–2
1990	Edmonton Oilers	Boston Bruins	4–1
1989	Calgary Flames	Montreal Canadiens	4–2
1988	Edmonton Oilers	Boston Bruins	4–0
1987	Edmonton Oilers	Philadelphia Flyers	4–3
1986	Montreal Canadiens	Calgary Flames	4–1
1985	Edmonton Oilers	Philadelphia Flyers	4–1

YEAR	CHAMPIONSHIPS	FINAL ROUND OPPONENT	GAMES
1984	Edmonton Oilers	New York Islanders	4–1
1983	New York Islanders	Edmonton Oilers	4–0
1982	New York Islanders	Vancouver Canucks	4–0
1981	New York Islanders	Minnesota North Stars	4–1
1980	New York Islanders	Philadelphia Flyers	4–2
1979	Montreal Canadiens	New York Rangers	4–1
1978	Montreal Canadiens	Boston Bruins	4–2
1977	Montreal Canadiens	Boston Bruins	4–0
1976	Montreal Canadiens	Philadelphia Flyers	4–0
1975	Philadelphia Flyers	Buffalo Sabres	4–2
1974	Philadelphia Flyers	Boston Bruins	4–2
1973	Montreal Canadiens	Chicago Black Hawks	4–2
1972	Boston Bruins	New York Rangers	4–2
1971	Montreal Canadiens	Chicago Black Hawks	4–3
1970	Boston Bruins	St. Louis Blues	4–0

YEAR	CHAMPIONSHIPS	FINAL ROUND OPPONENT	GAMES
1969	Montreal Canadiens	St. Louis Blues	4–0
1968	Montreal Canadiens	St. Louis Blues	4–0
1967	Toronto Maple Leafs	Montreal Canadiens	4–2
1966	Montreal Canadiens	Detroit Red Wings	4–2
1965	Montreal Canadiens	Chicago Black Hawks	4–3
1964	Toronto Maple Leafs	Detroit Red Wings	4–3
1963	Toronto Maple Leafs	Detroit Red Wings	4–1
1962	Toronto Maple Leafs	Chicago Black Hawks	4–2
1961	Chicago Black Hawks	Detroit Red Wings	4–2
1960	Montreal Canadiens	Toronto Maple Leafs	4–0
1959	Montreal Canadiens	Toronto Maple Leafs	4–1
1958	Montreal Canadiens	Boston Bruins	4–2
1957	Montreal Canadiens	Boston Bruins	4–1
1956	Montreal Canadiens	Detroit Red Wings	4–1
1955	Detroit Red Wings	Montreal Canadiens	4–3

YEAR	CHAMPIONSHIPS	FINAL ROUND OPPONENT	GAMES
1954	Detroit Red Wings	Montreal Canadiens	4–3
1953	Montreal Canadiens	Boston Bruins	4–1
1952	Detroit Red Wings	Montreal Canadiens	4–0
1951	Toronto Maple Leafs	Montreal Canadiens	4–1
1950	Detroit Red Wings	New York Rangers	4–3
1949	Toronto Maple Leafs	Detroit Red Wings	4–0
1948	Toronto Maple Leafs	Detroit Red Wings	4–0
1947	Toronto Maple Leafs	Montreal Canadiens	4–2
1946	Montreal Canadiens	Boston Bruins	4–1
1945	Toronto Maple Leafs	Detroit Red Wings	4–3
1944	Montreal Canadiens	Chicago Black Hawks	4–0
1943	Detroit Red Wings	Boston Bruins	4–0
1942	Toronto Maple Leafs	Detroit Red Wings	4–3
1941	Boston Bruins	Detroit Red Wings	4–0
1940	New York Rangers	Toronto Maple Leafs	4–2

YEAR	CHAMPIONSHIPS	FINAL ROUND OPPONENT	GAMES
1939	Boston Bruins	Toronto Maple Leafs	4–1
1938	Chicago Black Hawks	Toronto Maple Leafs	3–1
1937	Detroit Red Wings	New York Rangers	3–2
1936	Detroit Red Wings	Toronto Maple Leafs	3–1
1935	Montreal Maroons	Toronto Maple Leafs	3–0
1934	Chicago Black Hawks	Detroit Red Wings	3–1
1933	New York Rangers	Toronto Maple Leafs	3–1
1932	Toronto Maple Leafs	New York Rangers	3–0
1931	Montreal Canadiens	Chicago Black Hawks	3–2
1930	Montreal Canadiens	Boston Bruins	2–0
1929	Boston Bruins	New York Rangers	2–0
1928	New York Rangers	Montreal Maroons	3–2
1927	Ottawa Senators	Boston Bruins	2–0–2
1926	Montreal Maroons	Victoria Cougars	3–1
1925	Victoria Cougars	Montreal Canadiens	3–1

YEAR	CHAMPIONSHIPS	FINAL ROUND OPPONENT	GAMES
1924	Montreal Canadiens	Calgary Tigers	2–0 and Vancouver Maroons 2–0
1923	Ottawa Senators	Edmonton Eskimos	2–0 and Vancouver Maroons 3–1
1922	Toronto St. Pats	Vancouver Millionaires	3–2
1921	Ottawa Senators	Vancouver Millionaires	3–2
1920	Ottawa Senators	Seattle Metropolitans	3–2
1919	No decision. Montreal and Seattle tied 2–2–1. Series cancelled due to an influenza epidemic.		
1918	Toronto Arenas	Vancouver Millionaires	3–2

(NHL formed in 1917)

1917	Seattle Metropolitans
1916	Montreal Canadiens
1915	Vancouver Millionaires
1914	Toronto Blueshirts
1913	Quebec Bulldogs
1912	Quebec Bulldogs
1911	Ottawa Senators
1910	Montreal Wanderers
1909	Ottawa Senators
1908	Montreal Wanderers
1907	Montreal Wanderers (March)

1907	Kenora Thistles (January)
1906	Montreal Wanderers
1905	Ottawa Silver Seven
1904	Ottawa Silver Seven
1903	Ottawa Silver Seven
1902	Montreal Amateur Athletic Association
1901	Winnipeg Victorias
1900	Montreal Shamrocks
1899	Montreal Shamrocks
1898	Montreal Victorias
1897	Montreal Victorias
1896	Montreal Victorias (December)
1896	Winnipeg Victorias (February)
1895	Montreal Victorias
1894	Montreal Amateur Athletic Association
1893	Montreal Amateur Athletic Association

• •

HOCKEY PLAYERS: BEST EVER BY POSITION

Center: Wayne Gretzky
Left Wing: Bobby Hull
Right Wing: Gordie Howe
Defense: Bobby Orr
Defense: Brad Park
Goalie: Ken Dryden

PLUMBING, SCREWDRIVING, AND TWIST-OFF TOPS

Right is tight, left is loose. This motion is nearly universal. Turn accordingly.

PENIS SIZES

Biggest recorded: 18 inches (erect)
Smallest: 3 inches
Average length: 4 inches limp, 6 inches erect
Average girth, erect (distance around): 3.7 inches

Size is measured by taking your erect penis and measuring it along the top with a ruler. Press the ruler against your pubic bone, and then measure to the tip of your dick.

Girth is measured with a cloth tape.

MILITARY RANKS

SCALE	ARMY	AIR FORCE
Commissioned Officers		
Wartime	General of the Army	General of the Air Force
O-10	Army Chief of Staff	Air Force Chief of Staff
	General	General
O-9	Lieutenant General	Lieutenant General
O-8	Major General	Major General
O-7	Brigadier General	Brigadier General
O-6	Colonel	Colonel
O-5	Lieutenant Colonel	Lieutenant Colonel
O-4	Major	Major
O-3	Captain	Captain
O-2	1st Lieutenant	1st Lieutenant
O-1	2nd Lieutenant	2nd Lieutenant
Warrant Officers		
W-5	Master Warrant Officer 5	X
W-4	Chief Officer 4	X
W-3	Chief Officer 3	X
W-2	Chief Officer 2	X
W-1	Warrant Officer 1	X
Non-Commissioned Officer		
Special	Sergeant Major of the Army	Chief Master Sergeant of the Air Force
E-9	Command Sgt Major Sergeant Major	First Sergeant & Chief Master Sergeant
E-8	First Sergeant Master Sergeant	First Sergeant & Senior Master Sergeant
E-7	Sergeant First Class	First Sergeant & Master Sergeant
E-6	Staff Sergeant	Technical Sergeant
E-5	Sergeant	Staff Sergeant
Enlisted Personnel		
E-4	Corporal/Specialist	Senior Airman
E-3	Private First Class	Airman First Class
E-2	Private	Airman
E-1	Private (Recruit)	Airman Basic

MARINES

X
Commandant of the MC
General

Lieutenant General
Major General
Brigadier General
Colonel
Lieutenant Colonel
Major
Captain
1st Lieutenant
2nd Lieutenant

Master Warrant Officer 5
Chief Warrant Officer 4
Chief Warrant Officer 3
Chief Warrant Officer 2
Warrant Officer 1

Sergeant Major of the
   Marine Corps
Sergeant Major
Master Gunnery Sergeant
First Sergeant
Master Sergeant
Gunnery Sergeant
Staff Sergeant
Sergeant

Corporal
Lance Corporal
Private First Class
Private

NAVY AND COAST GUARD

Fleet Admiral
Chief of Naval Operations
Admiral
Commandant of the Coast Guard
Vice Admiral
Rear Admiral (Upper Half)
Rear Admiral (Commodore)
Captain
Commander
Lieutenant Commander
Lieutenant
Lieutenant, Junior Grade
Ensign

Master Warrant Officer 5
Chief Warrant Officer 4
Chief Warrant Officer 3
Chief Warrant Officer 2
Warrant Officer 1

Master Chief Petty Officer
   of the Navy
Master Chief Petty Officer

Senior Chief Petty Officer

Chief Petty Officer
Petty Officer First Class
Petty Officer Second Class

Petty Officer Third Class
Seaman
Seaman Apprentice
Seaman Recruit

HAIR, BUT NOT THERE

Here's a disheartening fact. As you get older, you will naturally lose hair on your head. Maybe a little, maybe a lot. Maybe all of it. The lucky ones just lose it up along their hairline, the unlucky will look like recipients of a bikini wax gone horribly wrong.

The converse of this, which is almost as painful, is that you will grow hair in places you absolutely don't want it. Science doesn't even know why. It usually happens when you're around forty, but it can happen a few years earlier or later. Regardless of age, it will happen. Where? Your nose (inside and out), your back, your ears, and your eyebrows. Back hair we can't make a recommendation about; that you'll have to deal with on your own (they have parlors that will do removal—with varying levels of pain). As for the others, here are the best ways to deal with it, short of going to see a professional.

Ear hair: Hair will grow on the outside of your ear, and in some cases in the inner ridges. Left unattended, it will make your ears look like Lon Chaney, Jr.'s, in *The Wolfman*. On him it looked cool. On everybody else it looks hideous. The remedy? Don't shave it. It'll just grow back—thicker. Instead, pluck it with tweezers. Yeah, it'll hurt, but not as much as the looks you'll get from women who wonder why your ears have begun to look like Lassie's.

Nose hair (internal): Unfortunately, you need the hair inside your nose to filter out a lot of the crap in the air before you breathe it into your lungs. It also helps keep mucous inside your nose. Without hair, it might as well be Teflon up there in your nostrils. So, you can either thin the hair out or trim it down. There are a few ways to do this. One is to use short scissors with rounded tips. They sell these in drug stores. The rounded tips keep you from inadvertently jabbing the point up through your nostril and out through your skin. Trust us; that is about as ugly an accident as it gets on your face. You can also buy special battery-powered trimmers that feature little tiny spinning blades that snip the hairs like a mini roto-rooter.

You can also tweeze them or pull them out with your fingertips, but this is pretty painful. You also don't want to pluck them to the point they won't grow back. The pain in and of itself should dissuade you. Little known secret: when actors need to quickly produce tears in their eyes, they often do it by pulling their nose hairs out. On second thought, it might be good to know this when your girlfriend tells you Fluffy died and you're trying to appear appropriately sympathetic.

The thing is, if you don't trim your nose hairs, they begin to droop out of your nostrils. Then they hang out over your lip, and people will want to grab them and yank them out on their own. So trim the hair before someone asks why you're growing a moustache in your nose.

Nose hair (external): There is only one way to get rid of these weird little hairs. Pluck them. If you don't want to, maybe you can audition to replace Jo Jo the Dog-faced Boy at the state fair.

Eyebrows: The weird thing about eyebrows is that you don't get more of them; they just grow longer. And longer and longer. The longer they get, the more directions they point. We've seen eyebrows that reach across the room. The guys who don't trim them don't notice, but everyone else sure as shit does. They look like a vine just waiting to strangle someone. The remedy? Trim them with scissors. Just brush your eyebrows upward with your fingers, and then cut them in a straight line across the top. Don't pluck them, because eventually they won't grow back and you'll look like a transvestite. And if you do pluck them, know in advance that it hurts like a son of a bitch. Pulling nose hairs will make you tear up, but pulling eyebrows might make you break down and sob.

Pubic Hair: Your pubes and chest hair will turn gray. And it will be as coarse and tough as steel wire. Leave it alone. It's going to change at its own rate—usually one at a time, which is extremely weird—so live with it.

• •

STAR TREK TIMELINE

2151–2: *Enterprise* season one. Captain Jonathon Archer and crew set off in the NX-01 *Enterprise*

2152–3: *Enterprise* season two

2155: Earth-Romulan war begins

2158: the transporter invented

2160: Earth-Romulan war ends

2161: beginning of the United Federation of Planets; Starfleet commissioned

2218: Klingons and humans make first contact

2267: *Star Trek* season one; chronicles of Captain James T. Kirk

2268: *Star Trek* season two

2269: *Star Trek* season three

2272: Kirk is promoted to admiral and Head of Starfleet Operations

2274: events of *Star Trek: The Motion Picture*

2290: Sulu gets command of *Excelsior*

2293: events of *Star Trek: The Undiscovered Country*, human/Klingon neutral zone abolished

2294: events of *Star Trek: Generations* (first part), *Enterprise-B* commissioned

2344: *Enterprise-C* destroyed

2364: *The Next Generation* season one; the adventures of Captain Jean Luc Picard

2365: *The Next Generation* season two

2366: *The Next Generation* season three

2367: *The Next Generation* season four

2368: *The Next Generation* season five

2369: *The Next Generation* season six; *Deep Space Nine* season one

2370: *The Next Generation* season seven; *Deep Space Nine* season two

2371: *Deep Space Nine* season three; *Voyager* season one; *Star Trek: Generations* (second part)

2372: *Deep Space Nine* season four; *Voyager* season two

2373: *Deep Space Nine* season five; *Voyager* season three; events of *Star Trek: First Contact*

2374: *Deep Space Nine* season six; *Voyager* season four

2375: *Deep Space Nine* season seven; *Voyager* season five
2376: *Voyager* season six
2379: events of *Star Trek Nemesis*

• •

SATELLITES AND SPACE

The scientifically defined starting point of space is 240 miles above Earth. This is the end of our atmosphere, technically known as the exosphere.

One hundred and three miles up is the minimum altitude at which a satellite can be kept in orbit. Objects orbiting at this height—including satellites and the space shuttle crews—have to travel at approximately 17,500 mph to stay aloft. A bullet shot from a high-powered rifle can briefly reach speeds of 1800 mph. Jet fighters can reach cruising speeds of over 1300 mph.

- Low-Earth orbit satellites (LEOs) are positioned between 250 and 500 miles over the Earth.
- Medium-Earth orbit satellites (MEOs) have an altitude ranging from several hundred miles on up to several thousand miles. GPS satellites are MEOs.
- Geostationary or geosynchronous orbit satellites (GEOs) hold a fixed—or geographically stationary—position above a specific point on the equator. This happens at an altitude of 22,300 miles. The majority of satellites are GEOs.

REAL NAMES OF FAMOUS GUYS

John Wayne: Marion Morrison
Rock Hudson: Roy Scherer
Kirk Douglas: Issur Danielovitch Demsky
Boris Karloff: William Pratt
Gene Simmons and Paul Stanley of KISS: Chaim Witz
    and Stanley Eisen
Tony Curtis: Bernard Schwartz
Cary Grant: Archibald Leach
Hulk Hogan: Terry Bolea
Ralph Lauren: Ralph Lipschitz
Dean Martin: Dino Crocetti
Steven Tyler of Aerosmith: Steven Tallarico
Rodney Dangerfield: Jacob Cohen

DESCRIBING A DUMBSHIT, PART 2

He reached rock bottom and has started to dig.
His men would follow him anywhere, but only out of
    morbid curiosity.
I would not allow this man to breed.
He is really not so much of a has-been, but more of a def-
    inite won't be.
Works well when under constant supervision and cor-
    nered like a rat in a trap.

When she opens her mouth, it seems that it is only to change feet.

He would be out of his depth in a parking lot puddle.

This young lady has delusions of adequacy.

He sets low personal standards and then consistently fails to achieve them.

He is depriving a village somewhere of an idiot.

He should go far, and the sooner he starts, the better.

Got a full six-pack, but lacks the plastic thing to hold it all together.

A gross ignoramus—144 times worse than an ordinary ignoramus.

He certainly takes a long time to make his pointless.

He doesn't have ulcers, but he's a carrier.

I would like to go hunting with him sometime.

He's been working with glue too much.

He would argue with a signpost.

He has a knack for making strangers immediately.

He brings a lot of joy whenever he leaves the room.

When his IQ reaches fifty, he should sell.

If you see two people talking and one looks bored, he's the other one.

A photographic memory but with the lens cover glued on.

A prime candidate for natural deselection.

Donated his brain to science before he was done using it.

Has two brains; one is lost and the other is out looking for it.

MARCH MADNESS

NCAA Division I Men's Basketball Championship

The first national championship basketball tournament was held in 1939 with eight teams. The final game was played in Evanston, Illinois, and Oregon defeated Ohio State. Games were not televised until 1946.

There are 310 teams in Division I, most of which are concentrated in 31 divisions. The winners of March conference tournaments in these 31 divisions receive automatic bids to the championships (the exceptions are PAC-10 and Ivy League conferences, which send "best record" teams). An additional 34 teams from other conferences will get at-large bids. Truthfully, no one but the NCAA understands completely how these 34 get chosen. This brings the total to 64 teams. Those teams are then invited "to the dance."

They are divided into four brackets: East, South, West, Midwest.

Single eliminations over the course of the month—the finals are actually in April—lead to these matchups:

Sweet Sixteen
Elite Eight
Final Four
Champion

THE MOST DESIRABLE WOMEN IN HISTORY

Cleopatra
Helen of Troy
Sophia Lauren
Audrey Hepburn
Grace Kelly
Marilyn Monroe

LEPRECHAUNS

A guy is taking a leak at a urinal when he looks over at the midget next to him taking a leak. He notices the midget's dick is the size of a large kielbasa sausage. "Wow," he says in amazement. "Sorry to bother you, but I'm impressed. You have an enormous dick," he tells the midget.

"That's because I'm a leprechaun," the midget says. "I use this dick to grant wishes."

"Really?" says the man, interested. "What kind of wishes?"

"Well, anyone who lets me stick my dick up their ass gets any wish they want."

The man is repulsed, and says, "No way, thanks anyway. That's not for me."

The leprechaun shrugs and says, "That's okay. Your loss."

As the guy walks out of the bathroom and back to his office, he stops. *You know,* he tells himself, *for a hundred million dollars I could quit this job. And all it would take would be a quick bone up the ass. And no one would ever know.*

He hurries back into the bathroom, and grabs the leprechaun. "I'll do it," he says. "But I want a hundred million dollars."

"Done!" says the leprechaun. "Why don't we go into this stall, where it's a little more private?"

The guy hesitates and then decides to do it. He drops his pants and bends over. Suddenly, the full weight of the kielbasa-sized dick is thrust into him. The guy grunts in pain, but reminds himself it's all for a hundred million dollars.

As the leprechaun is thrusting away, he decides to make small talk. "So, what be your name, laddie?"

"Bill!" the guy moans, barely able to talk from the pain in his rectum.

"And how old might ye be there, Bill?"

Bill feels like he is choking on the leprechaun's dick from the inside out. "Twenty-seven years old!" he shouts.

The leprechaun nods, getting ready to plunge in for the money shot.

"Now Bill," he says with a final thrust, "aren't ye a wee bit old to be believing in leprechauns?"

YOUR WARDROBE

Your clothes are a matter of taste. Some guys will spend thousands of dollars on Armani suits, while others can rule the world dressed in jeans and a T-shirt. Your style is yours, so we won't try to dictate it. However, there is one thing all men who are preparing for marriage, or are entering into a long-term relationship, should know: You didn't know anything about dressing yourself before you got married.

Regardless of what you think, or how stylish you may be, you were a fashion flop in the great dressing room of life before your significant other got ahold of you. It doesn't matter how tastefully you dress, or how current you are with your subscription to *Esquire* magazine. Prior to marriage, you were a dressing dunce.

Don't argue. We don't care if you worked at Neiman Marcus since you were a child. We don't care if you were raised by fashion coordinators from Neiman Marcus since birth. We don't even care if you were raised *by* Neiman Marcus, right in the middle of the men's department. You *did not* know anything about dressing properly until you got married. If you chose it yourself, and put it on your body, it was, and is, a fashion faux pas. Even if you picked your wardrobe piece by meticulous piece out of the most fashionable menswear catalog in the entire world, your wife will dismiss it by saying, "Do you really want to wear that belt with that shirt?" This is a subtle, yet effective put-down she will employ that is meant to make you question your fashion sense—without her looking like the bad guy or even just a nag.

Of course, you could say what you really feel in

response to this question, like, "No, I don't really want to wear this belt with this *shirt*. I want to wear this belt with these *pants*," or, "No, I don't really want to wear this belt with this shirt, but some genetic defect and brain deformity compels me to." But you *won't* do this. Instead, you will act like a lamb—being led to slaughter—and respond, "Why? Doesn't the belt go with the shirt?"

Because you have replied, you are done for. Now you are trapped, because whether the belt goes with the shirt or not is *not* the issue. Not even close. What is the issue is that your wife already had something else in mind for you to wear, and by starting with a little innocuous remark about your belt—which is admittedly one of the least important aspects of your wardrobe—she can get you to change every item of clothing over to the ensemble she had in mind for you when you decided you were going out for the evening.

For instance, you could wear your favorite suit—with your favorite tie and socks—as an unmarried person, and draw rave reviews from many women regarding your individuality, your sense of style, and your fashion sense. But the minute you wear that same suit after you are married, this same clothes combination turns into a horrible abomination that needs to be taken out and destroyed, preferably by an ordained priest or a witch doctor, lest you ever wear it in public. This is true even if you marry one of the women that once gave you rave reviews on it before. So an important thing to remember regarding suits and other public wear: Do not, I repeat, do not attempt to dress yourself for formal occasions after your second month of marriage. It can only lead to trouble, heartbreak, and social embarrassment. Not for you, of course, but for your wife. Truth be told, you probably couldn't give a shit one way or the other.

As far as wives are concerned, their husbands can fuck up the basic coordination involved in putting on a pair of jeans and a T-shirt. This is trivial, yet true. You may think your wife is going to mention the fact that your Metallica T-shirt is inappropriate for a company picnic, so you offset it with your best pair of jeans, planning to head her off at the pass and avoid a clothes "discussion." A safe bet, right?

Wrong. There is no safe bet. Your wife will say, "Why don't you wear those black jeans we bought last week with that shirt?" You will want to say that they are still in the bag with the tags on them, that they haven't been washed, etc. Don't even dare. Because if you had already put on the black jeans to start with, she would say, "Aren't those a little too 'dressy to wear with a T-shirt?" You would still be on the short end of an already shortened stick. And even though we are talking about basic black, a color combination that even blind people can put together successfully, your wife will think you dress like somebody who learned color coordination from Ringling Brothers, not Brooks Brothers.

You will not win a fashion confrontation, so don't try. The odds against you are astounding. You have a better chance of breaking the bank at Caesar's Palace on the quarter slots than you do of winning a fashion confrontation with God's Designated Fashion Gestapo—your wife.

Fashion arguments are exactly the kind of trivial situation that have caused many men to walk into crowded buildings carrying a loaded semiautomatic weapon with the clips full and the safety off. So save yourself the stress. Put on whatever your wife wants you to. You'll live longer, and if you live longer than she does, then you can dress any goddamned way you please after that.

• •

PLAYMATES OF THE YEAR

YEAR	NAME	AGE	BIRTHDATE
1960	Ellen Stratton	(20)	Jun 9, 1939
1961	Linda Gamble	(20)	Sep 11, 1939
1962	Christa Speck	(19)	Aug 1, 1942
1963	June Cochran	(20)	Feb 2, 1942
1964	Donna Michelle	(17)	Dec 8, 1945
1965	Jo Collins	(19)	Aug 5, 1945
1966	Allison Parks	(21)	Oct 18, 1943
1967	Lisa Baker	(21)	Mar 19, 1945
1968	Angela Dorian	(22)	Sep 26, 1944
1969	Connie Kreski	(20)	Sep 19, 1946
1970	Claudia Jennings	(19)	Dec 20, 1949
1971	Sharon Olivia Clark	(26)	Oct 15, 1943
1972	Liv Lindeland	(25)	Dec 7, 1945
1973	Marilyn Cole	(22)	May 7, 1949
1974	Cyndi Wood	(22)	Sep 25, 1950
1975	Marilyn Lange	(22)	Jan 12, 1952
1976	Lillian Muller	(19)	Aug 19, 1952
1977	Patti McGuire	(25)	Sep 5, 1951
1978	Debra Jo Fondren	(22)	Feb 5, 1955
1979	Monique St. Pierre	(24)	Nov 25, 1953
1980	Dorothy Stratten	(19)	Feb 28, 1960

YEAR	NAME	AGE	BIRTHDATE
1981	Terri Welles	(24)	Nov 21, 1956
1982	Shannon Lee Tweed	(24)	Mar 10, 1957
1983	Marianne Gravatte	(22)	Dec 13, 1959
1984	Barbara L. Edwards	(23)	Jun 26, 1960
1985	Karen Velez	(23)	Jan 27, 1961
1986	Kathy Ann Shower	(32)	Mar 8, 1953
1987	Donna Edmondson	(20)	Feb 1, 1966
1988	India Allen	(22)	Jun 1, 1965
1989	Kimberley Conrad	(24)	Aug 6, 1963
1990	Renee Tenison	(20)	Dec 2, 1968
1991	Lisa Matthews	(20)	Sep 24, 1969
1992	Corinna D. Harney	(19)	Feb 20, 1972
1993	Anna Nicole Smith	(24)	Nov 28, 1967
1994	Jenny McCarthy	(20)	Nov 1, 1972
1995	Julie Lynn Cialini	(23)	Nov 14, 1970
1996	Stacy Sanches	(21)	Sep 4, 1973
1997	Victoria Silvstedt	(22)	Sep 19, 1974
1998	Karen McDougal	(26)	Mar 23, 1971
1999	Heather Kozar	(21)	May 4, 1976
2000	Jodi Ann Paterson	(24)	Jul 31, 1975
2001	Brande Nicole Roderick	(27)	Jun 13, 1974
2002	Dalene Kurtis	(24)	Nov 12, 1977
2003	Christina Santiago	(21)	Oct 15, 1981
2004	Carmella DeCesare	(21)	July 1,1982
2005	Tiffany Fallon	(30)	May 1, 1974
2006	Kara Monaco	(23)	February 26, 1983
2007	Sara Jean Underwood	(23)	March 26, 1984

Ages have ranged from 17 (Donna Michelle in 1964) to 32 (Kathy Ann Shower in 1986). Average age is 22 years old.

POP STARS AND SUPERMODELS

What is it with pop stars and supermodels? In the real world, most of these guys couldn't get laid with a fistful of hundreds in a two-dollar whorehouse. And their careers invariably go downhill once they start hanging out with these women.

Billy Joel & Christie Brinkley (divorced)
Mick Jagger & Jerry Hall (divorced)
Tommy Lee & Pam Anderson (divorced)
Kid Rock & Pam Anderson (divorced)
Tommy Lee & Heather Locklear (divorced)
Richie Sambora & Heather Locklear (divorced)
Ric Ocasek & Paulina Poriskova (married)
Axl Rose & Stephanie Seymour (dated)
Harry Connick, Jr., & Jill Goodacre (married)
Rod Stewart & Rachel Hunter (divorced)
Ringo Starr & Barbara Bach (married)
Nikki Sixx & Donna D'Errico (divorced)
John Cougar Mellencamp & Elaine Erwin (married)
David Bowie & Iman (married)
Keith Richards & Patty Hanson (living together)

THE BEST DUMB BLONDE JOKES

Q: *How do blonde brain cells die?*
A: Alone.

Q: *Why do blondes get confused in the ladies' room?*
A: They have to pull their own pants down.

Q: *Why do blondes wear panties?*
A: To keep their ankles warm.

Q: *Why did the blonde stare at the frozen orange juice can for two hours?*
A: Because it said "concentrate."

Q: *What is the first thing a blonde learns when she takes driving lessons?*
A: You can also sit upright in a car.

Q: *What is the difference between blondes and traffic signs?*
A: Some traffic signs say stop.

Q: *What's the difference between a blonde and a lightbulb?*
A: The lightbulb is smarter, but the blonde is easier to turn on.

Q: *What's the difference between a blonde and a bitch?*
A: A blonde will fuck anyone, a bitch will fuck anyone but you.

Q: *How does the blonde turn on the light after she has had sex?*
A: She opens the car door.

Q: *What did the blonde do when she heard the British were coming?*
A: She stopped sucking.

Q: *What job function does a blonde have in an M&M factory?*
A: Proofreading.

Q: *Do you know why the blonde got fired from the M&M factory?*
A: For throwing out the Ws.

Q: *What does a blonde say after multiple orgasms?*
A: Way to go team!

Q: *Did you hear about the conceited blonde?*
A: She screams her own name when she comes.

Q: *Did you hear about the blonde that robbed a bank?*
A: She tied up the safe and blew the guard.

Q: *Why don't blondes talk while having sex?*
A1: Their mothers told them not to talk to strangers.
A2: Their mothers told them not to talk with their mouths full.

Q: *How can you tell if a blonde's been using the computer?*
A: There's Wite-Out on the screen.

Q: *How can you tell if another blonde's been using the computer?*
A: There's writing on the Wite-Out.

Q: *What's the difference between a blonde and a computer?*
A: You only have to punch information into a computer once.

Q: *Why is 68 the maximum speed for blonds?*
A: Because at 69 they blow a rod . . .

Q: *What's a blonde's idea of safe sex?*
A: Locking the car door.

Q: *Did you hear about the blonde who tried to blow up her husband's car?*

A: She burned her lips on the tailpipe.

Q: *What does a blonde put behind her ears to make her more attractive?*

A: Her ankles.

Q: *What do you see when you look into a blonde's eyes?*

A: The back of her skull.

HOW TO HOT-WIRE A CAR

You see it on TV and in movies, and you read about it in books: some average guy is on the run from ninja-level

killers and is out of options. At the last possible moment, he decides to hot-wire a car and escapes his grisly fate.

Who the fuck are these guys that know how to hot-wire a car? It's not like they teach it in driver's ed or show you at the dealership when you're buying a new vehicle. For most of us, the answer to the question, "When was the last time you hot-wired a car?" is "Never." But knowing how to hot-wire can come in handy for those times when you've lost your keys, or broken them off in the ignition, or need to exit a tense situation and your own car is not available. Not that we're suggesting doing anything illegal, but in a life-and-death situation, you pretty much want to avoid the death side of the equation.

Here are the basics.

1) Just like the goddamned "know-it-alls" in the movies do, get on the floor of the driver's side and look up under the dash. You'll find five wires leading up to the ignition switch. (If the ignition switch is in the steering column, open the column by wedging a screwdriver between the steering wheel and the column and plying the casing off the column.)

2) Pull all five wires off the ignition switch (some modes only have four wires). Make sure you have some exposed wiring; if not, strip off some of the casing with a knife or your thumbnail. Remember, some of these will be live when they connect to each other, so be careful where you put your fingers.

3) There should be two matching wires (usually red, but not always). Touch these together, and you'll get electrical power into the car. Two wires down, three to go.

4) Keeping the first two touching each other, touch the other wires ONE AT A TIME to the combined color pair. You're looking for the starter wire. If there's a brown or black wire, start with that one. When you touch the right one to the combined pair, the engine should start right up.

5) Once the engine is running, take the starter wire away from the combined pair. Push the three non-matching wires away from each other as they could spark and give you a shock if they touch.

BASEBALL WORLD SERIES

YEAR	WINNER	LOSER	SERIES
1901	American and National Leagues refuse to play one another		
1902	American and National Leagues refuse to play one another		
1903	Boston Red Sox	Pittsburgh Pirates	5–3
1904	NY Giants manager John McGraw refuses to play AL team		
1905	New York Giants	Philadelphia Athletics	4–1
1906	Chicago White Sox	Chicago Cubs	4–2
1907	Chicago Cubs	Detroit Tigers	4–0 (one tie)
1908	Chicago Cubs	Detroit Tigers	4–1
1909	Pittsburgh Pirates	Detroit Tigers	4–3

YEAR	WINNER	LOSER	SERIES
1910	Philadelphia Athletics	Chicago Cubs	4–1
1911	Philadelphia Athletics	New York Giants	4–2
1912	Boston Red Sox	New York Giants	4–3 (one tie)
1913	Philadelphia Athletics	New York Giants	4–1
1914	Boston Braves	Philadelphia Athletics	4–0
1915	Boston Red Sox	Philadelphia Phillies	4–1
1916	Boston Red Sox	Brooklyn Robins	4–1
1917	Chicago White Sox	New York Giants	4–2
1918	Boston Red Sox	Chicago Cubs	4–2
1919	Cincinnati Reds	Chicago White Sox	5–3
1920	Cleveland Indians	Brooklyn Robins	5–2
1921	New York Giants	New York Yankees	5–3
1922	New York Giants	New York Yankees	4–0
1923	New York Yankees	New York Giants	4–2
1924	Washington Senators	New York Giants	4–3
1925	Pittsburgh Pirates	Washington Senators	4–3
1926	St. Louis Cardinals	New York Yankees	4–3
1927	New York Yankees	Pittsburgh Pirates	4–0

YEAR	WINNER	LOSER	SERIES
1928	New York Yankees	St. Louis Cardinals	4–0
1929	Philadelphia Athletics	Chicago Cubs	4–1
1930	Philadelphia Athletics	St. Louis Cardinals	4–2
1931	St. Louis Cardinals	Philadelphia Athletics	4–3
1932	New York Yankees	Chicago Cubs	4–0
1933	New York Giants	Washington Senators	4–1
1934	St. Louis Cardinals	Detroit Tigers	4–3
1935	Detroit Tigers	Chicago Cubs	4–2
1936	New York Yankees	New York Giants	4–2
1937	New York Yankees	New York Giants	4–1
1938	New York Yankees	Chicago Cubs	4–0
1939	New York Yankees	Cincinnati Reds	4–0
1940	Cincinnati Reds	Detroit Tigers	4–3
1941	New York Yankees	Brooklyn Dodgers	4–1
1942	St. Louis Cardinals	New York Yankees	4–1
1943	New York Yankees	St. Louis Cardinals	4–1

YEAR	WINNER	LOSER	SERIES
1944	St. Louis Cardinals	St. Louis Browns	4–2
1945	Detroit Tigers	Chicago Cubs	4–3
1946	St. Louis Cardinals	Boston Red Sox	4–3
1947	New York Yankees	Brooklyn Dodgers	4–3
1948	Cleveland Indians	Boston Braves	4–2
1949	New York Yankees	Brooklyn Dodgers	4–1
1950	New York Yankees	Philadelphia Phillies	4–0
1951	New York Yankees	New York Giants	4–2
1952	New York Yankees	Brooklyn Dodgers	4–3
1953	New York Yankees	Brooklyn Dodgers	4–2
1954	New York Giants	Cleveland Indians	4–0
1955	Brooklyn Dodgers	New York Yankees	4–3
1956	New York Yankees	Brooklyn Dodgers	4–3
1957	Milwaukee Braves	New York Yankees	4–3
1958	New York Yankees	Milwaukee Braves	4–3
1959	Los Angeles Dodgers	Chicago White Sox	4–2

YEAR	WINNER	LOSER	SERIES
1960	Pittsburgh Pirates	New York Yankees	4–3
1961	New York Yankees	Cincinnati Reds	4–1
1962	New York Yankees	San Francisco Giants	4–3
1963	Los Angeles Dodgers	New York Yankees	4–0
1964	St. Louis Cardinals	New York Yankees	4–3
1965	Los Angeles Dodgers	Minnesota Twins	4–3
1966	Baltimore Orioles	Los Angeles Dodgers	4–0
1967	St. Louis Cardinals	Boston Red Sox	4–3
1968	Detroit Tigers	St. Louis Cardinals	4–3
1969	New York Mets	Baltimore Orioles	4–1
1970	Baltimore Orioles	Cincinnati Reds	4–1
1971	Pittsburgh Pirates	Baltimore Orioles	4–3
1972	Oakland Athletics	Cincinnati Reds	4–3
1973	Oakland Athletics	New York Mets	4–3
1974	Oakland Athletics	Los Angeles Dodgers	4–1
1975	Cincinnati Reds	Boston Red Sox	4–3

YEAR	WINNER	LOSER	SERIES
1976	Cincinnati Reds	New York Yankees	4–0
1977	New York Yankees	Los Angeles Dodgers	4–2
1978	New York Yankees	Los Angeles Dodgers	4–2
1979	Pittsburgh Pirates	Baltimore Orioles	4–3
1980	Philadelphia Phillies	Kansas City Royals	4–2
1981	Los Angeles Dodgers	New York Yankees	4–2
1982	St. Louis Cardinals	Milwaukee Brewers	4–3
1983	Baltimore Orioles	Philadelphia Phillies	4–1
1984	Detroit Tigers	San Diego Padres	4–1
1985	Kansas City Royals	St. Louis Cardinals	4–3
1986	New York Mets	Boston Red Sox	4–3
1987	Minnesota Twins	St. Louis Cardinals	4–3
1988	Los Angeles Dodgers	Oakland Athletics	4–1
1989	Oakland Athletics	San Francisco Giants	4–0
1990	Cincinnati Reds	Oakland Athletics	4–0
1991	Minnesota Twins	Atlanta Braves	4–3

YEAR	WINNER	LOSER	SERIES
1992	Toronto Blue Jays	Atlanta Braves	4–2
1993	Toronto Blue Jays	Philadelphia Phillies	4–2
1994	No World Series, player's strike		
1995	Atlanta Braves	Cleveland Indians	4–1
1996	New York Yankees	Atlanta Braves	4–2
1997	Florida Marlins	Cleveland Indians	4–3
1998	New York Yankees	San Diego Padres	4–0
1999	New York Yankees	Atlanta Braves	4–0
2000	New York Yankees	New York Mets	4–1
2001	Arizona Diamondbacks	New York Yankees	4–3
2002	Anaheim Angels	San Francisco Giants	4–3
2003	Florida Marlins	New York Yankees	4–2
2004	Boston Red Sox	St. Louis Cardinals	4–0
2005	Chicago White Sox	Houston Astros	4–0
2006	St. Louis Cardinals	Detroit Tigers	4–1
2007	Boston Red Sox	Colorado Rockies	4–0

WORLD SERIES MVPS

YEAR	PLAYER & TEAM	PERFORMANCE
2007	Mike Lowell, Boston	.400, 1 HR, 4 RBI
2006	David Eckstein, St. Louis	.363, 4 RBI
2005	Jermaine Dye, Chicago	.438, 1 HR, 3 RBI
2004	Manny Ramirez, Boston	.412, 1 HR, 4 RBI
2003	Josh Becket, Florida	1–1, 1.13 ERA, 16.1 IP, 19K
2002	Troy Glaus, Anaheim	.385, 3 HR, 8 RBI
2001	Randy Johnson & Curt Schilling, Arizona	RJ: 3–0, 1.04, 17 IP, 19K / CS: 1–0, 1.69, 21 IP, 26K
2000	Derek Jeter, New York (AL)	.409, 2 RBI, 2 HR, 2 2B, 1 3B
1999	Mariano Rivera, New York (AL)	4.2 IP, 1 W, 2 S, 1 BB, 3 SO
1998	Scott Brosius, New York (AL)	.471, 2 HR, 6 RBI
1997	Livan Hernandez, Florida	2–0, 13.2 IP, 7 K

YEAR	PLAYER & TEAM	PERFORMANCE
1996	John Wetteland, New York (AL)	5 G, 4 Saves, 4.1 IP, 6 K
1995	Tom Glavine, Atlanta	2–0, 1.29, 14 IP, 11 K
1994	not held, season cancelled	
1993	Paul Molitor, Toronto	.500, 2 2B, 2 3B, 2 HR, 8 RBI
1992	Pat Borders, Toronto	.450, 3 2B, 1 HR, 3 RBI
1991	Jack Morris, Minnesota	2–0, 1.17 ERA, 23 IP, 15 K
1990	Jose Rijo, Cincinnati	2–0, 0.59 ERA, 15.1 IP, 5 K
1989	Dave Stewart, Oakland	2–0, 1.69 ERA, 16 IP, 14 K
1988	Orel Hershiser, Los Angeles	2–0, 1.00 ERA, 18 IP, 17 K
1987	Frank Viola, Minnesota	2–1, 3.72 ERA, 19.1 IP, 16 K
1986	Ray Knight, New York (NL)	.391, 1 2B, 1 HR, 5 RBI
1985	Bret Saberhagen, Kansas City	2–0, 0.50 ERA, 18 IP, 10 K
1984	Alan Trammell, Detroit	.450, 1 2B, 2 HR, 6 RBI
1983	Rick Dempsey, Baltimore	.385, 4 2B, 1 HR, 2 RBI
1982	Darrell Porter, St. Louis	.286, 2 2B, 1 HR, 5 RBI
1981	Ron Cey, Los Angeles	.350, 1 HR, 6 RBI

YEAR	PLAYER & TEAM	PERFORMANCE
1981	Pedro Guerrero, Los Angeles	.333, 1 2B, 1 3B, 2 HR, 7 RBI
1981	Steve Yeager, Los Angeles	.286, 1 2B, 2 HR, 4 RBI
1980	Mike Schmidt, Philadelphia	.381, 1 2B, 2 HR, 7 RBI
1979	Willie Stargell, Pittsburgh	.400, 4 2B, 3 HR, 7 RBI
1978	Bucky Dent, New York (AL)	.417, 1 2B, 7 RBI
1977	Reggie Jackson, New York (AL)	.450, 5 HR, 8 RBI
1976	Johnny Bench, Cincinnati	.533, 1 2B, 1 3B, 2 HR, 6 RBI
1975	Pete Rose, Cincinnati	.370, 3 R, 1 2B, 1 3B, 2 RBI
1974	Rollie Fingers, Oakland	1–0, 2 SV, 1.93, 6 K
1973	Reggie Jackson, Oakland	.310, 3 2B, 1 3B, 1 HR, 6 RBI
1972	Gene Tenace, Oakland	.348, 4 HR, 9 RBI
1971	Roberto Clemente, Pittsburgh	.414, 2 2B, 1 3B, 2 HR, 4 RBI
1970	Brooks Robinson, Baltimore	.429, 2 2B, 2 HR, 6 RBI
1969	Donn Clendenon, New York (NL)	.357, 3 HR, 4 RBI
1968	Mickey Lolich, Detroit	3–0, 1.67 ERA, 27 IP, 21 K

YEAR	PLAYER & TEAM	PERFORMANCE
1967	Bob Gibson, St. Louis	3–0, 1.00 ERA, 27 IP, 26 K
1966	Frank Robinson, Baltimore	.286, 1 3B, 2 HR, 3 RBI
1965	Sandy Koufax, Los Angeles	2–1, 0.38 ERA, 24 IP, 29 K
1964	Bob Gibson, St. Louis	2–1, 3.00 ERA, 27 IP, 31 K
1963	Sandy Koufax, Los Angeles	2–0, 1.50 ERA, 18 IP, 23 K
1962	Ralph Terry, New York (AL)	2–1, 1.80 ERA, 16 K
1961	Whitey Ford, New York (AL)	2–0, 0.00 ERA, 7 K
1960	Bobby Richardson, New York (AL)	1 HR, 2 2B, 2 3B, 12 RBI
1959	Larry Sherry, Los Angeles	2–0, 0.71 ERA
1958	Bob Turley, New York (AL)	2–1, 2.76 ERA, 13 K
1957	Lew Burdette, Milwaukee (NL)	3–0, 0.67 ERA, 13 K
1956	Don Larsen, New York (AL)	Perfect Game, 7 K
1955	Johnny Podres, Brooklyn	2–0, 1.00 ERA, 2 CG

MLB PERFECT GAMES

A perfect game is one in which no opposing player reaches first base, either by a base hit, base on balls, hit batter, or fielding error. Thus, the pitcher or pitchers retire all 27 opposing batters in order. It is both a no-hitter and a shutout.

DATE	PITCHER	TEAM	OPPONENT	SCORE
4/5/1904	Cy Young	BOS	PHI	3–0
8/11/1907	Ed Karger	STL	BOS	4–0 Called after 7
10/5/1907	Rube Vickers	PHI	WAS	4–0 Called after 5
10/2/1908	Addie Joss	CLE	CHI	1–0
4/30/1922	Charlie Robertson	CHI	DET	1–0
10/8/1956	Don Larsen	NYY	BRK	2–0 Postseason
6/21/1964	Jim Bunning	PHI	NYM	6–0
9/9/1965	Sandy Koufax	LA	CHI	1–0
8/6/1967	Dean Chance	MIN	STL	2–0 Called after 5
5/8/1968	Catfish Hunter	OAK	MIN	4–0
5/15/1981	Len Barker	CLE	TOR	3–0
4/21/1984	David Palmer	MTL	STL	4–0 Called after 5
9/30/1984	Mike Witt	CAL	TEX	1–0
9/16/1988	Tom Browning	CIN	LA	1–0

DATE	PITCHER	TEAM	OPPONENT	SCORE
7/28/1991	Dennis Martinez	MTL	LA	2–0
7/28/1994	Kenny Rogers	TEX	CAL	4–0
5/17/1998	David Wells	NYY	MIN	4–0
7/18/1999	David Cone	NYY	MTL	6–0
5/18/2004	Randy Johnson	AZ	ATL	2–0

• •

WINDOW TREATMENTS

Look around you, wherever you may happen to be at this moment. Unless you are living in a cave—which is where your wife thinks you lived before you met her—there is probably a window in the room you're in.

What do you see near that window? Curtains? Drapes? Shades? Blinds? Miniblinds? Venetian blinds? Blind Venetians? You may see all of these things, but you are actually seeing none of them. That is because you are uninformed. What you are looking at is technically called a "window treatment."

You never knew that before, but now you do. And by the way, window treatments can be very expensive, so be prepared. This is one of the most unexpected elements of home ownership, from a guy's perspective, but women see it as an essential home feature. Just like a toilet and a TV.

YO MAMA

Yo mama so ugly when she joined an ugly contest, they said, "Sorry, no professionals."

Yo mama so ugly they filmed *Gorillas in the Mist* in her shower.

Yo mama so stupid it took her two hours to watch *60 Minutes*.

Yo mama so stupid she told everyone that she was "illegitimate" because she couldn't read.

Yo mama so stupid she watches *The Three Stooges* and takes notes.

Yo mama so nasty I called her for phone sex and she gave me an ear infection.

Yo mama so lazy she thinks a two-income family is where yo daddy has two jobs.

Yo mama so fat her nickname is "DAMN!"

Yo mama so fat when the bitch goes to an all-you-can-eat buffet, they have to install speed bumps.

Yo mama so fat when she steps on a scale, it reads "one at a time, please."

Yo mama so fat she had to go to Sea World to get baptized.

Yo mama so fat she got to iron her pants on the driveway.

1000 WORDS FOR BREASTS

A

airbags • all-day suckers • Alps • amazons • ample supply • angel cakes • Appalachians • apple dumpling shops • apples • altars • artichokes • assets • atom smashers • attic • areolae borealis • advantages • avocados • awning

B

B-52s • babaloos • baby baits • baby feeders • baby's best friend • baby's dinner • baby's public house • Babylons • back rubbers • backbreakers • backrests • bag of groceries • baggies • baggos • bags • bajungas • balboas • balcony • ballistics • balloons • baloobas • banana squeezers • bangers • bangles • banzais • baps • barnacles • barrels • basketballs • bassoons • bath toys • batons • battleships • baubles • bazongas • bazonkers • bazookas • bazooms • bazoombas • beach balls • beacons • beanbags • beaters • bebops • bedtime beach balls • bee stings • begonias • Berthas • best friends • Betties • big bazooties • big Berthas • big boppers • big brown eyes • big foot radials • big sacks of jugs • big 'uns • big guns • bijongas • bikini stuffers • billibongs • binoculars • bio domes • biscuits • bits of tits • bitties • bizcochos • blimps • blockbusters • blouse bunnies • bobos • bodacious ta-tas • boingos • bolshy groodies • bongos • bonkers • boobage • boobolas • boobalicious • boobers • boobies • booblets • booblies • boobs • boobules • booby • bookends • book rests • bombs • boomers • boom-

boom rockets • bosoms • Boston wobblers • bottles • boulders • bouncers • bouncing beauties • bouncing Betties • bounders • boy bait • boys • bozos • bra buddies • bra busters • bra fight • bra stuffers • Braunsteins • breakfast tray • breasteses • breasticles • brisket • bronads • Bronskis • Bronx Bombers • brown-speckled pups • brown-nosed sweater puppies • brownies • bubbas • bubbies • bubble cups • bubbles • bubs • buckets • buds • bulbs • bulges • bullets • bumper cars • bumper guards • bumpers • bumps • bumps in the night • bumpy bits • bunnies • buoys • bushels • bushel bubbies • bust • busters • bustieres • busties • busts • bustular substances • butter bags • butterballs • buttons

C

cabambas • caboodles • cachongas • Cadillac bumpers • cafe la mama • calabazas • Camelots • candy dispenser machine • cams • canisters • cannonballs • cannons • cans • cantaloupes • capitol domes • car waxers • caracas • carumbas • casaba melons • casabas • castanets • castles in the air • cha-chas • chachabingos • chalupas • Charlie's Angels • chaw • chee chees • cheek warmers • cherry cakes • cherry caps • chest • chest armor • chest fat • chest hams • chest meat • chest ornaments • chest pillows • chest puppies • chest zeppelins • Chesterfields • chesticles • chestnuts • chi-chis • chicharrones • chickadees • chickaroonies • chihuahuas • chimichangas • chimpanzees • chiquitas • chock blocks • chockey-nips • chokers • choochoos • chombalonies • chubbies • chubs • chumbawumbas • chungas • cinch sacks • circus tents • clams • cleft udders • coat hangers • coconuts • cock warmers • cold weather indicators • combreastables •

commode cloggers • comfort fruits • concitas • cones • congas • continental shelf • cookies • corkers • cowabungas • creamers • cream pies • cream puffs • crowd pleasers • cruise missiles • cubs • cuddly dudes • cuhuangas • cupcakes • cups • cups-runneth-over • curves • cushions

D

da-das • dactylic delights • dagmars • dairy • dairy makers • dairy pillows • dandies • danglers • dangling participles • delicate orbs of womanhood • demigods • desperados • dessert • devil's dumplings • dick mashers • dick massagers • dick parking • dick rollers • diddies • ding dongs • dingers • dinghies • dinglebobbers • dingoes • dinners • dirigibles • dirty pillows • distributor caps • domes • donkey's ears • doodads • doorbells • doorknobs • doozers • doozies • doppelgangers • double dribbles • double Ds • double trouble • double whammies • doudounes • doughboys • droopers • drums • dual air bags • dual floppies • duckies • deuce-and-a-halves • dueling banjos • dugs • dum dums • dumbbells • dumplings • dunes • durantes • Dutch Alps • dynamic duo • dynamite

E

earmuffs • eclairs • eggplants • eggs • egos • Eigers • el primo torpedoes • elephants • enchiladas • Epcots • Ericas • erotic volcanoes • explosives • eyes • eye slappers

F

face pillows • fat bags • fat storage • feed bags • flapjacks • flappers • flat plains • flesh balloons • flesh bulbs • flesh-

colored fun bags • flesh fillets • flesh Fuji • flesh melons •
floaters • floats • flopdoodles • floppers • flotation
devices • flowers of attitude • flyswatters • fog lights • food
for thought • footlights • Fortress of Breastitude • fried
eggs • friends • front-end alignment • front porch • frontal
elevation • frontal female water wings • frosties • fry-
babies • Fujiyamas • fun bags • fun bubs • fun bubbles •
fun domes • funsters • funnel cakes

G

gagas • gajoombas • gajungas • garbage bags • garbanzos •
Garbos • gazingas • gazelles • gazongas • gazungas •
gazoombas • geegees • geminis • girls • girlie bumpers •
girlie guns • girl thangs • glad bags • glands • glandular en-
dowments • globelets • globes • glockenspiels • gobstop-
pers • God's greatest creation • God's milk bottles •
Godzillas • golden bozos • golden domes • golden globes •
gongas • goobers • good bits • goodies • Goodyears •
goombas • grab-'ems • grapefruits • gravity magnets •
great galloping galoogies • great wobbling wazoo-
bies • gribnacks • grillwork • grips • groodies • groupies
• guavas • gumballs • gumdrops • gunboats • guns

H

ha ha's • hakuna mutatas • hallelujahs • ham curtains •
hammers • hammocks for two • handfuls • handlebars •
handholds • handsets • hand warmers • hangers • hanging cucumbers • happy bags • happy pillows • happy
sacks • happy-fun-squeezy-friends • hat hangers • head-
bangers • headers • headlamps • headlights • headphones
• headsets • healthy set of lungs • heavers • heavy-duty

honeydews • heavy hangers • hee-haws • hefties • heifers • helicopters • hematomas • hemispheres • Hershey's kisses • high beams • high pockets • high-rise weather balloons • hills • Himalayas • Hindenburgs • hinderbinders • hippos • ho hos • hobey J's • hogans • home sweet home • honeydews • honey holders • honkers • hood ornaments • hoohas • hoohoos • hoosiers • hooters • hoots • hoovers • horns • hot-air balloons • hot commodities • hotcakes • hottentots • the hounds • House of Lords • howitzers • howlers • hubba bubbas • hubcaps • huffies • hug bumps • huge maguffies • huggy bears • human tetherballs • humdingers • humonganoids • humping hooters • hurricane lanterns • Hush Puppies • hypnotizers

I

I-want-thems • ICBMs • ice caps • ice cream scoops • ice cubes • Idahos • igloos • implants • inflatables • Isaac Newtons • itty bits

J

jackalopes • jackanapes • jacks • jaggers • jahoobies • jambalayas • jawbreakers • jelly bells • Jemimas • jets • jibs • jigglies • jigglers • jiggly wigglies • jobbers • jubblies • juggernauts • juggies • jugglies • jugs • jukes • jumblies • jumbo chickpeas • jumbos

K

kabombas • kajoobies • kalamazoos • kawangas • kayaks • kazongas • kazoos • keepers • kettle drums • kiwis • knickknacks • knobbers • knobs • knockers • kongas • krunks • kumquats

L

La Breas • lactating lungs • lactation station • lactic lobes • lacto grenades • lactoids • lady bumps • lady lumps • lampoons • launch codes • lean-to's • lefty 'n' righty • lemons • lethal weapons • leverage • lewd muffins • lightbulbs • Lindas • lip fodder • little duckies • llamas • load stones • loaves • loaves of love • lobes • loblollies • lolas • lollies • lollipops • lollos • lolos • long-range tanks • lookers • loomas • lost sheep • love balloons • love handles • love jugs • love kegs • love lumps • love melons • love muffins • love pillows • lovelies • low riders • lucky charms • lug 'ems • lulas • lung covers • lung hammers • lung humps • lung nuts • lungs • lung warts

M

macaroons • mackerels • Madonnas • magnates • magnets • magnificent pontoons of love • magookins • maguppies • Mahatmas • majestic mountains • major guns • major-league yabos • major motion picture material • male-madness inducers • mamacitas • mama's pillows • mambazos • mambajahambas • mammalian protuberances • mammaries • mammary glands • Mammary Lane • mammies • mams • mammoth mounds o' fun • man magnets • man puppets • mangos • man"nip"ulators • maracas • marangos • maraschinos • marbles • margaritas • marimbas • marshmallows • massage pillows • matching headlights • mau-maus • Mausers • mazongas • McFloppities • McGees • meat bags • meatballs • meat loaves • meat miracles • meat pillows • melon patch • melons • mesmerizers • milk bags • milk bladders • milk bombs • milk bottles • milk cans • Milk Duds • milk fountains • milk jugs • milk kegs • milk makers • milk melons • milk miracles • milk shakes • milk towers • milk wagons • milky sacks of calcium • milky moos • milky sways • Mimis • minarets • minesweepers • minnebagos • missiles • Miss Left and Right • Mobutus • mogambas • mojubas • mommas • mommy bags • mondos • moneymakers • Monroes • Montezumas • moo moos • moogies • moon pies • moonlight sonatas • mosobs • mother lodes • mounds • mounds of Jell-O • mountain peaks • mountains • Mount Fujis • mouthwatering scoops of flesh • moveable feast • muchachas • muffins • mulligans • Murphies • mushmelons

N

*National Geographic*s • nature's airbags • nature's founts • nature's little thermometers • naughty bits • naughty pillows • nay-nays • nectarines • neeners • nefertitties • neh-neh • never nevers • niblets • nibs • nice set of hands • nice-uns • nin-nins • ninnies • ninny jugs • nipple-caddies • nipple-odeon • nipple sundaes • nodes • nodules • noochies • noogies • noonies • norkies • norks • northern neon-beamed headlights • nortons • nose cones • nuclear warheads • nuggs • nummy juggs • nunga nungas • nukes

O

obelisks • oblations • oboes • omigods • oompas • Oppenheimers • oracles • orbs • ostrich eggs • ottomans • overhang • overstuffed cushions

P

padding • paducahs • pagodas • pair • pair of problems • palms • palko • palookas • Pamelas • pancakes • papayas • parabolas • parrots • party bags • party hats • party passes • pastor baiters • pastries • paw patties • peaches • peacocks • peakers • peaks • pears • pebbles • pects • peepers • pencil erasers • pendulums • penis pillows • perkies • perkos • perpetual entertainment • personal flotation devices • pies • Pike's Peaks • pillows • pimples • ping pings • pink-nosed puppies • pinkies • pips • planetoids • pleasant eminences • pleasure mounds • pleasure peaks • pleasure pouches • plentifuls • plums • plumpers • plumpies • pneumatic bliss • pods of lust • pokers • polygons • pompoms • ponderosas • pontoons • popinjays • portable typewriters • potatoes • praise Gods • presidential pair • pretty-pretties • professors • proof that God exists • protuberances • PT boats • pumpkin patch • pumpkins • pumps • punching bags • puppies • pushmatahas • pyramids

Q

Quakers • quantities • quantum heaps • quasars • queen-missiles • quit-its

R

rack • rackage • radar domes • radials • raisins • Ralph Waldo Emersons • rampolenes • Rangoons • Raquels • raspberry ripples • reasons to live • red carpets • rib balloons • rib bumpers • rib cushions • rib flaps • rivets • rockets • Rockies • rositas • rotors • rotundas grandes •

roundabouts • roundies • roundtrippers • round mounds
of get down • ruby reds • Rudolphs

S

saggers • saggies • salamanders • sams • samosas •
sandbags • Sapphos • satellites • schooners • scones •
Scooby snacks • scoops • scud missiles • searchlights •
second-base set • shabba-dos • shakers • Shebas •
shelf • Shermans • Sherman tanks • shimmies • shirt
potatoes • shirt stuffers • shock absorbers • shoe
buffers • show stoppers • Sierra Madres • silos • silver
stars • sin pillows • sisters • skeeter bites • ski slopes •
ski slopes to Heaven • skin sacks • slappers • slutskers •
smart set • smoothies • smuggling raisins • snack rack •
snack trays • snoogans • snootchie bootchie nootchies •
snorbs • snow cones • snow tires • snowy promi-
nences • snuggle pups • softies • sopapillas • space
aliens • spark plugs • specials • speed bags • speed
bumps • spheres • spinaroonies • splazoingas • sponge
cakes • spontaneous combustibles • spooge buttons •
spuds • squashers • squeaky toys • stacks • stash in the
dash • stocking stuffers • strap tangers • stratus-
spheres • stress busters • stripper's ATMs • stuff • stuffing • stun grenades • sturgeons • sucklebags • sugar
cubes • sugar melons • sugarplums • super droopers •
supernauts • sultanas • sweater bumpers • sweater
cows • sweater kittens • sweater meat • sweater melons • sweater mittens • sweater monkeys • sweater pillows • sweater puffs • sweater puppets • sweater
puppies • sweater stuffers • sweat glands • sweet rolls

T

ta-tas • Tahitis • talents • tallapoosas • tamales • tambourines • tankers • tassels • tasty cakes • tater tots • tats • tatters • tatties • tattlers • teacups • teatolas • teats • teepees • teetees • teeters • tentacles • terrible twos • terrible twosome • Tetons • thangs • thank yous • thingamajigs • thingamajugs • thingbies • thingies • things • thoughtful orbs • thirty-eights • thwackers • ticket punchers • ticket sellers • tidbits • tig bitties • time stoppers • time zones • ti-ots • tippers • titbits • tits • titskis • titter • titties • Titticacas • titty tats • TNT • tobacco pouch • tomatoes • tom-toms • tongue depressors • tongue twisters • tonsils • tool bags • tooters • Tootsie Pops • top bollocks • top heavy • Tora Boras • torpedo • Tortugas • totos • totties • towers • towering twin peaks • tracts of land • traffic stoppers • treasure • tribbles • triple Ds • turaluras • twangers • tweakers • tweeters • twin cities • twin flagships of her majesty's royal navy • twin mounds • twin peaks • the twins • two puppies in a burlap bag • twofers • tympanis • type 2s

U

U-boats • udders • Uhurus • umbrellas • umlauts • umpa loompas • unidentified bouncing objects • upper karoos • USDAs

V

Van Dorens • victrolas • volcanoes • volumes • Volvos

W

wah-wah pedals • wabs • wahwahs • Waldos • Wally Jumblatts • Wally wispoppers • Walters • warheads • warts • water balloons • watermelons • weapons • weapons of mass distraction • weapons of mass erection • whamdanglers • whammers • whapoons • whatchamacall'ems • whim whams • white rabbits • whoo-hoos • whoopies • whoppers • wibbly wobbly wonders • wide bodies • wigglers • wigwams • Wilsons • windbags • windjammers • windmills • windshield wipers • Winnebagos • wipers • wobblers • wobbly-bobbly fun bags • womanpecs • womanhood • wonder twins • wonderments • wongas • wonkas • woodymakers • woofers • wookies • wopbopaloobops • workbench • World Trade Centers • wows • wreaths

X

xenoliths • X-rateds

Y

yabbahos • yabbos • yabos • yahoos • yahtzees • yam bags • yams • yayas • yazoos • yeast dough • ying yangs • yippies • yitties • Yolandas • yomamas • Yoo-hoos • yowsers • yubees • yum-yums • yummies • yugos

Z

Z-bras • zeppelins • ziggurats • Ziggys • zingers • zippys • zonkers • zoom zooms • zoombas • zoomers • zwiebacks

SUPERHEROES AND THEIR SECRET IDENTITIES

DC COMICS

Superman	Clark Kent
Batman	Bruce Wayne
Robin	Dick Grayson
Green Lantern	Alan Scott
Wonder Woman	Diana Prince
Aquaman	Arthur Curry
The Flash	Jay Garrick
Plastic Man	Eel O'Brien
Hawkman	Carter Hall

MARVEL COMICS

Spider-Man	Peter Parker
Thor	Dr. Donald Blake
Iron Man	Tony Stark
Submariner	Namor McKenzie
The Hulk	Dr. Bruce Banner
Daredevil	Matt Murdock
Captain America	Steve Rogers
Hawkeye	Clint Barton

The Fantastic Four:

Mr. Fantastic	Reed Richards
The Human Torch	Johnny Storm
Invisible Woman	Susan Storm Richards
The Thing	Ben Grim

THE OLDER WOMEN: COUGARS AND MILFS

History has long driven young men to want older women, and old men to want younger women. It's a scenario played out all over the world and from generation to generation. It's a lot like the circle of life, except with heavy petting and lubricants.

Older men will find trophy wives and gold diggers only after they've become financially successful—and old. Being old is a requisite condition we can't do anything about, so we're going to address the needs of younger men here. That means describing two categories of older women: Cougars and MILFs.

COUGARS

If you want to do it with an older woman, the Cougar is at your service. An aggressive sex-starved predator with an engorged libido, this middle-aged maniac will deliver it to your bed . . . and then tuck you in. Typically a divorced woman with a little bit of spending money, a lot of free nights, and a sex drive with no brakes, her only interest is in meeting young guys who will make her rip the sheets just like when she was a teenager. Oh, and those guys better be good in bed, because the Cougar is in it for the orgasms, not the relationship.

A notable subset of Cougars are Trolling Teachers. These are the married, yet babalicious, middle school and high school teachers who take an active sexual interest in their very young students. While climbing into the backseat of Dad's SUV with your incredibly hot geography teacher is in the top five of all male fantasies, it turns out that it's illegal for the Trolling Teacher to do this. That puts a bit of a damper on the whole affair. Besides, once you're too old to go to high school PE class, the Trolling Teacher will most likely view you as little more than a senior citizen with a shriveled-up penis—even if you're only nineteen.

MILFS

The "Mom I'd Like to Fuck." Think Donna Reed in *It's a Wonderful Life*, think Barbara Billingsley in *Leave It to Beaver*, think Rachel Hunter climbing out of the pool in that "Stacy's Mom" music video. There's a MILF on every young guy's list, but unfortunately MILFs are more fantasy than reality. The MILF is usually a friend's mother, but could be one of the smoking-hot neighborhood moms with a couple of little kids at home. In truth, the odds of getting a MILF are almost nonexistent. Most guys will have to go for a Cougar, whose own kids are probably already in college.

•••••••••••••••••••••••••••••

WHO WOULD WIN?

These are fights to the death, knock-down drag-outs to determine the champions once and for all. It'll take a lot of beers and a lot of dead brain cells, but the answers are out there.

Great white shark vs. a grizzly bear

Batman vs. Spider-Man

Samantha Stevens of *Bewitched* vs. Jeannie of *I Dream of Jeannie*

Muhammad Ali vs. Mike Tyson

Alien vs. Predator

Star Trek vs. *Battlestar Galactica*

Rocky vs. Rambo

David Lee Roth vs. Sammy Hagar

Captain Kirk vs. Captain Picard

Wonder Woman vs. Super Girl

John Lennon vs. Mick Jagger

Yoko Ono vs. Linda McCartney

Linda McCartney vs. Heather Mills McCartney

Mike Ditka vs. Bill Parcells

Chuck Norris vs. Bruce Lee

Robocop vs. The Six Million Dollar Man

Hillary Clinton vs. Bill Clinton

Pamela Anderson vs. Raquel Welch

Jay Leno vs. David Letterman

Jackie Chan vs. Bruce Lee

Spawn vs. Hellboy

Al Pacino vs. Robert De Niro

Teddy Roosevelt vs. John F. Kennedy

Merlin vs. Gandalf vs. Dumbledore

Jason Bourne vs. James Bond

Superman vs. Jesus

OTTO DeFAY is a freelance writer and sports-data analyst who spends most of his life on the road and in semidecent hotels. Among his notable achievements are scoring a hole-in-one at the Russian Jack Springs Golf Course in Anchorage, Alaska, and breaking three ribs during a layup in the final four seconds of his high school basketball championship. He has not dated anybody famous—yet—but he did win $17,550 once while playing blackjack in Las Vegas. This is his first book.